JUDGMENT DAY AT THE WHITE HOUSE

Judgment Day
at the White House

*A Critical Declaration Exploring Moral Issues
and the Political Use and Abuse of Religion*

Edited by

Gabriel Fackre

William B. Eerdmans Publishing Company
Grand Rapids, Michigan / Cambridge, U.K.

© 1999 Wm. B. Eerdmans Publishing Co.
255 Jefferson Ave. S.E., Grand Rapids, Michigan 49503 /
P.O. Box 163, Cambridge CB3 9PU U.K.

Printed in the United States of America

04 03 02 01 00 99   7 6 5 4 3 2 1

Library of Congress Cataloging-in-Publication Data

ISBN 0-8028-4671-8

Contents

PART I
DECLARATION SIGNATORIES MAKE THEIR CASE

Section A
The Ethics and Politics of Repentance and Forgiveness

Contents

Section B
Biblical, Pastoral, and Theological Perspectives on Public Morality

PART II
DECLARATION CRITICS RESPOND

Contents

PART III
NATIONAL COLUMNISTS SPEAK OUT

PART IV
PRESIDENT CLINTON ON THE RECORD

Preface

This is an improbable book. Conceived in September by the formulators of the "Declaration," taken on by an imaginative publisher in October, essays solicited and received in November, and into the bookstores in December?

The cause of the alacrity was the rush of events. As the designers of *Judgment Day at the White House,* we believed that another word needed to be spoken in a conversation too fast closing. We have been troubled by both the high-profile religious pleas to "forgive and forget" and by the war cries of the Religious Right. Reflections by teachers of religion and ethics on a subject touching their own disciplines were in order, we believed. Especially so from scholars who have long histories of commitment to social justice and public morality as well as a concern for personal virtue. The framework would become the "Declaration concerning Religion, Ethics, and the Crisis in the Clinton Presidency" — a dissent from popular opinion. We felt that this book should contain criticisms of the Declaration and a civil conversation along with the interpretations of the Declaration's signers.

The volume begins with the Declaration. Originally drafted by New Testament scholars, it has been revised in response to feedback and signed by more than 140 teachers and writers. Part I is made up of essays by signatories of the Declaration. The first chapter of Part I, Section A, is by political ethicist Jean Bethke Elshtain, whose counsel has been invaluable throughout. The first chapter under Part I, Section B, is the most detailed, and rightly so, for it was written by Robert Jewett, the chief facilitator of an overall project that includes the Declaration, this book, and an Internet website (http://www.moral-crisis.org). The rest of Part I is composed of contributions based on the premises of the Declaration.

Part II includes essays by those who have written on matters of personal and public morality but have chosen not to sign the Declaration and, indeed, are critical of it on various counts. Part III reprints essays by Stephen Carter, Andrew Sullivan, and Shelby Steele that originally appeared elsewhere and parallel the Declaration's concerns. Part IV reprints President Clinton's televised address to the nation on August 17, 1998, and his speech at the Religious Leaders' Prayer Breakfast on September 11, 1998.

The question of impeachment may be moot by the time most readers get to these pages. But the issues posed by the presidential crisis will be with us for a long time to come. As will the witness to the inseparability of personal and public morality that drives the Declaration and brought this volume to be.

Gabriel Fackre
Advent 1998

Declaration concerning Religion, Ethics, and the Crisis in the Clinton Presidency

As scholars interested in religion and public life, we protest the manipulation of religion and the debasing of moral language in the discussion about presidential responsibility. We believe that serious misunderstandings of repentance and forgiveness are being exploited for political advantage. The resulting moral confusion is a threat to the integrity of American religion and to the foundations of a civil society. In the conviction that politics and morality cannot be separated, we consider the current crisis to be a critical moment in the life of our country and, therefore, offer the following points for consideration:

1. Many of us worry about the political misuse of religion and religious symbols even as we endorse the public mission of our churches, synagogues, and mosques. In particular, we are concerned about the distortion that can come by association with presidential power in events such as the Presidential Prayer Breakfast of September 11, 1998. We fear that the religious community is in danger of being called upon to provide authentication for a politically motivated and incomplete repentance that seeks to avert serious consequences for wrongful acts. While we affirm that pastoral counseling sessions are an appropriate, confidential

1

arena in which to address these issues, we fear that announcing such meetings to convince the public of the President's sincerity compromises the integrity of religion.

2. We challenge the widespread assumption that forgiveness relieves a person of further responsibility and serious consequences. We are convinced that forgiveness is a relational term that does not function easily within the sphere of constitutional accountability. A wronged party chooses forgiveness instead of revenge and antagonism, but this does not relieve the wrongdoer of consequences. When the President continues to deny any liability for the sins he has confessed, it suggests that his public display of repentance was intended to avoid political disfavor.

3. We are aware that certain moral qualities are central to the survival of our political system, among which are truthfulness, integrity, respect for the law, respect for the dignity of others, adherence to the constitutional process, and a willingness to avoid the abuse of power. We reject the premise that violations of these ethical standards should be excused so long as a leader remains loyal to a particular political agenda and the nation is blessed by a strong economy. Elected leaders are accountable to the Constitution and to the people who elected them. By his own admission, the President has departed from ethical standards by abusing his presidential office, by his ill use of women, and by his knowing manipulation of truth for indefensible ends. We are particularly troubled about the debasing of the language of public discourse with the aim of avoiding responsibility for one's actions.

4. We are concerned about the impact of this crisis on our children and on our students. Some of them feel betrayed by a President in whom they set their hopes, while others are troubled by his misuse of others, by which many in the administration, the political system, and the media were implicated in patterns of deceit and abuse. Neither we nor our students demand perfection. Many of us believe that extreme dangers sometimes require a political leader to engage in morally problematic actions. But we maintain that in general there is a reasonable threshold of behavior beneath which our public leaders should not fall, because the moral character of a people is more important than the tenure of a particular politician or the protection of a particular political agenda. Political and religious history indicate that violations and misunder-

standings of such moral issues may have grave consequences. The widespread desire to "get this behind us" does not take seriously enough the nature of transgressions and their social effects.

5. We urge the society as a whole to take account of the ethical commitments necessary for a civil society and to seek the integrity of both public and private morality. While partisan conflicts have usually dominated past debates over public morality, we now confront a much deeper crisis: whether the moral basis of the constitutional system itself will be lost. In the present impeachment discussions, we call for national courage in deliberation that avoids ideological division and engages the process as a constitutional and ethical imperative. We ask Congress to discharge its current duty in a manner mindful of its solemn constitutional and political responsibilities. Only in this way can the process serve the good of the nation as a whole and avoid further sensationalism.

6. While some of us think that a presidential resignation or impeachment would be appropriate and others envision less drastic consequences, we are all convinced that extended discussion about constitutional, ethical, and religious issues will be required to clarify the situation and to make a wise decision possible. We hope to provide an arena in which such discussion can occur in an atmosphere of scholarly integrity and civility without partisan bias.

Signers of the Declaration

Scholars Interested in Religion and Public Life

December 1, 1998

Paul J. Achtemeier   *Union Theological Seminary in Virginia*
P. Mark Achtemeier   *University of Dubuque Theological Seminary*
LeRoy Aden   *Lutheran Theological Seminary in Philadelphia*
Diogenes Allen   *Princeton Theological Seminary*
Joseph Alulis   *North Park University*
Mark Appold   *Truman State University*
Warren Ashworth   *Pacific Union College*
David W. Baker   *Ashland Theological Seminary*
Charles L. Bartow   *Princeton Theological Seminary*
Todd S. Beall   *Capital Bible Seminary*
Michael S. Beates   *Reformed Theological Seminary at Orlando*
Linda L. Belleville   *North Park Theological Seminary*
Jeffrey P. Bjorck   *Fuller Theological Seminary*
Donald G. Bloesch   *University of Dubuque Theological Seminary*
Carl E. Braaten   *Center for Catholic and Evangelical Theology*
Grace Adolphsen Brame   *LaSalle University*
Manfred T. Brauch   *Eastern Baptist Theological Seminary*
Robert L. Brawley   *McCormick Theological Seminary*
William P. Brown   *Union Theological Seminary in Virginia*
Don S. Browning   *University of Chicago*
Frederick S. Carney   *Southern Methodist University*
Ellen T. Charry   *Princeton Theological Seminary*
Angela Russell Christman   *Loyola College in Maryland*

4

Signers of the Declaration

A. J. Conyers   *Baylor University*
D. Lyle Dabney   *Marquette University*
Karl Paul Donfried   *Smith College*
Richard Drummond   *University of Dubuque Theological Seminary*
Lenore T. Ealy   *Writer/Consultant, Carmel, IN*
Jean Bethke Elshtain   *University of Chicago*
Edward E. Ericson, Jr.   *Calvin College*
Gabriel J. Fackre   *Andover Newton Theological School*
Lareta Halteman Finger   *Messiah College*
Thomas Finger   *Eastern Mennonite Seminary*
Timothy E. Fulop   *King College*
Robert A. J. Gagnon   *Pittsburgh Theological Seminary*
Larry T. Geraty   *La Sierra University*
Mike Garrett   *New Orleans Baptist Theological Seminary*
Thomas W. Gillespie   *Princeton Theological Seminary*
W. Edward Glenny   *Central Baptist Seminary*
Russell W. Gough   *Pepperdine University*
Garrett Green   *Connecticut College*
Joel B. Green   *Asbury Theological Seminary*
Wayne Grudem   *Trinity Evangelical Divinity School*
Robert H. Gundry   *Westmont College*
David P. Gushee   *Union University*
Scott J. Hafemann   *Wheaton College*
Stanley S. Harakas   *Holy Cross Greek Orthodox School of Theology, Emeritus*
Roy A. Harrisville   *Luther Seminary*
Barry A. Harvey   *Baylor University*
Stanley M. Hauerwas   *The Divinity School, Duke University*
L. Daniel Hawk   *Ashland Theological Seminary*
Gerald F. Hawthorne   *Wheaton College*
David M. Hay   *Coe College*
Richard B. Hays   *The Divinity School, Duke University*
S. Mark Heim   *Andover Newton Theological School*
Charles E. Hill   *Reformed Theological Seminary at Orlando*
Christopher Thomas Hodgkins   *University of North Carolina at Greensboro*
Stephen C. Holmgren   *Nashotah House*
Frank Witt Hughes   *Codrington College*
L. D. Hurst   *University of California, Davis*
Mark Husbands   *University of St. Michael's College*
Robert Peter Imbelli   *Boston College*
Philip Jamieson   *Elyria United Methodist Church*
Robert W. Jenson   *Center for Theological Inquiry*
Robert Jewett   *Garrett-Evangelical Theological Seminary*

5

Signers of the Declaration

Thomas F. Johnson   *George Fox University*
Robert M. Johnston   *Andrews University*
L. Gregory Jones   *The Divinity School, Duke University*
Peter Jones   *Westminster Theological Seminary in California*
Jack Dean Kingsbury   *Union Theological Seminary in Virginia*
Paul E. Koptak   *North Park Theological Seminary*
Peter Kuzmic   *Gordon-Conwell Theological Seminary*
James LaGrand   *Beacon Light Church, Gary, IN*
Matthew L. Lamb   *Boston College*
Duane H. Larson   *Lutheran Theological Seminary at Gettysburg*
John S. Lawrence   *Morningside College*
Paul Leggett   *Grace Presbyterian Church, Montclair, NJ*
Walter L. Liefeld   *Trinity Evangelical Divinity School*
Benjamin Leslie   *North American Baptist Seminary*
Duane Stephen Long   *Garrett-Evangelical Theological Seminary*
Newton Malony   *School of Psychology, Fuller Theological Seminary*
R. Todd Mangum   *Biblical Theological Seminary*
Elmer A. Martens   *Mennonite Brethren Biblical Seminary*
Troy W. Martin   *Saint Xavier University*
James L. Mays   *Union Theological Seminary in Virginia*
S. Dean McBride, Jr.   *Union Theological Seminary in Virginia*
James McClanahan   *King College*
Sheila E. McGinn   *John Carroll University*
John R. McRay   *Wheaton College*
John McVay   *Andrews University*
Gary T. Meadors   *Grand Rapids Baptist Seminary*
Gilbert Meilaender   *Valparaiso University*
Eugene H. Merrill   *Dallas Theological Seminary*
Robert P. Meye   *Fuller Theological Seminary*
Kenneth H. Miller   *Evangelical School of Theology*
David P. Moessner   *University of Dubuque Theological Seminary*
Robert Mounce   *Whitworth College*
Carol M. Norén   *North Park Theological Seminary*
Grant R. Osborne   *Trinity Evangelical Divinity School*
Carroll D. Osburn   *Abilene Christian University*
Daniel C. Palm   *Azusa Pacific University*
William A. Pannell   *Fuller Theological Seminary*
Jon Paulien   *Andrews University*
John Piper   *Bethlehem Baptist Church*
Stephen J. Pope   *Boston College*
Janet Everts Powers   *Hope College*
Mark Reasoner   *Bethel College*

6

Signers of the Declaration

Thomas C. Reeves *University of Wisconsin-Parkside*
John Reumann *Lutheran Theological Seminary at Philadelphia, Emeritus*
David M. Rhoads *Lutheran School of Theology at Chicago*
W. Larry Richards *Andrews University*
Daniel E. Ritchie *Bethel College*
Joel Samuels *University of Dubuque Theological Seminary*
David M. Scholer *Fuller Theological Seminary*
Keith Norman Schoville *University of Wisconsin*
Richard Schultz *Wheaton College*
J. Julius Scott *Wheaton College*
Mark A. Seifrid *Southern Baptist Theological Seminary*
Christopher R. Seitz *St. Andrews University*
Klyne Snodgrass *North Park Theological Seminary*
Eric O. Springsted *Princeton Theological Seminary*
Max L. Stackhouse *Princeton Theological Seminary*
Calvin Stapert *Calvin College*
W. Richard Stegner *Garrett-Evangelical Theological Seminary*
K. James Stein *Garrett-Evangelical Theological Seminary*
Jeanne Stevenson-Moessner *University of Dubuque Theological Seminary*
R. Franklin Terry *Morningside College*
H. O. Tom Thomas *Asbury Theological Seminary*
J. Robert Vannoy *Biblical Theological Seminary*
Warren Wade *North Park University*
J. Ross Wagner *Princeton Theological Seminary*
David H. Wallace *American Baptist Seminary of the West*
Timothy P. Weber *Northern Baptist Theological Seminary*
Merold Westphal *Fordham University*
Woodrow Whidden *Andrews University*
Jonathan R. Wilson *Westmont College*
Anne Streaty Wimberly *Interdenominational Theological Center*
Edward P. Wimberly *Interdenominational Theological Center*
Harry Yeide *George Washington University*
Amos Yong *Bethany College*
Carl E. Zylstra *Dordt College*

PART I

Declaration Signatories
Make Their Case

SECTION A
The Ethics and Politics of Repentance and Forgiveness

Politics and Forgiveness:
The Clinton Case

JEAN BETHKE ELSHTAIN

We are awash in confession these days. There is the low form on daytime television talk shows and the slightly higher form in bookstores. Rectitude in personal matters has given way to "contrition chic," as one wag called it, meaning a bargain-basement way to gain publicity, sympathy, and even absolution by trafficking in one's status as victim or victimizer. Given the shameless nature of so much of our popular culture and the way it traffics in and cheapens notions of forgiveness ("let's get this behind us," "let's move to closure"), it would be tempting to end the matter right here and to dismiss all acts of public contrition as bogus.

But that doesn't seem right. Rather, what is required is to distinguish between instances of contrition chic and, by contrast, serious acts of public or political forgiveness. That is a first step. A second is to examine clearheadedly and tough-mindedly the relationship between contrition and forgiveness and the rule of law. When the person seeking forgiveness is not simply a "private" person but the holder of an office, what rules should pertain in evaluating when forgiveness wipes the slate clean, so to speak, and when it is but one moment in a more complex process in which legal and political consequences may also be involved?

Although individual acts of forgiveness — one human being to another — most often take place outside the full glare of publicity, there are others that are noteworthy for embodying a radical alternative to

11

contrition chic. One thinks here of Pope John Paul II, who, having barely survived an assassin's bullets, uttered his first public words from his hospital bed to the violent shooter whom he now described as "my brother, whom I have sincerely forgiven," words that preceded the pope's extraordinary visit to his brother and would-be killer in jail once he was up and about. There is a *gravitas* manifest in this narrative that is altogether lacking in American quasi-therapeutic, talk-showish confessions that are most often blatantly self-exculpatory in contrast to the way one professes a demanding faith — Christianity, in this instance — a faith within which forgiveness is a constitutive dimension.

Those for whom forgiveness is central and solemn engage in what theologian L. Gregory Jones calls the practice or "craft" of forgiveness in his recent book *Embodying Forgiveness: A Theological Analysis.* Pope John Paul II was practicing this craft and, in so doing, displaying to the world the ways in which forgiveness is not primarily about a singular confessional moment but about an enactment within a particular way of life, a way of life shaped not by foggy sentimentalism but by certain hard-won and difficult truths.[1] Moreover, forgiveness is something quite different from aloofness or detachment — just not giving a damn — also mistakenly presented nowadays as a form of forgiveness. What is at stake, then, is a tougher discipline by far than are public acts of easy repentance sought and something like "forgiveness" as a kind of willed amnesia proffered. When people sincerely try to make amends, it would be churlish of us to withhold from them any possibility that what they say or do might make a difference in, and for, the future. True. But the public repentance of a political figure cannot simply be a matter of words. Words and deeds cannot be so readily disentangled. And forgiveness still leaves open or unresolved a whole series of difficult political and legal questions related to the person's carrying out the duties of his or her office.

---

1. See Gerhard Forde, "On Being a Theologian of the Cross," *Christian Century* (October 22, 1997, pp. 947-49) for a discussion of why a theology of the cross is not about sentimentalism but about sin, redemption, punishment, reconciliation, God's justice, and so on. Forde worries that much contemporary language spoken from the pulpit has taken on all the coloration of the wider, sentimentalized surround, the mentality of "I'm okay, you're okay, everybody gets a pass." This turns the church into a support group "rather than the gathering of the body of Christ where the word of the cross and resurrection is proclaimed and heard."

Enter President Clinton and the sorry scandal that simultaneously transfixes us and invites an epidemic of denial. Why do we so much want all of this to "go away"? The answer, I believe, is complex and touches on our understanding of forgiveness, the rule of law, the proper demarcation between public and private, the nature of political office, and our responsibilities as citizens. These are inherently complex matters that do not lend themselves to sound bytes and simplistic — or moralistic, for that matter — resolutions. I shall address but a few.

First, the impeachment hearings now underway did not come about because the President exercised deplorable judgment in his "private" life. What goes on in the Oval Office is not enveloped within a private *cordon sanitaire*. Those who hold to this view insist that anything to do with sexuality is by conceptual fiat in a "zone of privacy," so why shouldn't this pertain in the President's case? There are legal, political, and theological responses. One of the things we have learned from three decades of feminism — and should have understood on grounds of simple decency all along — is that many serious offenses can be papered over with the claim that what went on is "nobody's business" but that of the participants involved. Sometimes, indeed, this is the case. But it is a mistake to argue that anything that can be filed under the rubric of "consent" is off limits to critical scrutiny. Let's assume that President Clinton and Ms. Lewinsky both "consented" to the relationship, if indeed what was going on can be thus characterized. Consent is no magic wand. Nagging questions remain, and serious problems are not automatically erased. Was this wise? Was it decent? Was it reckless? Was it damaging to all involved, consent or no consent?

Now take matters one step further. The relationship, or the provision of sexual services, involved employer and employee and took place in his — the employer's — place of work, which also happens to be one of the "sacred" sites of America's civic-minded people. One can hardly imagine a more public place in which to carry on intimate transactions. This was no "discreet affair," with the two principals doing their utmost to try to protect the feelings, the moral concerns, and the sensitivities of all involved. In addition, a small army of staffers was enlisted by the President to facilitate these assignations and an even larger number to cover matters up once things turned sour. Surely this has crossed the boundary into the public domain on every possible scale — ethical, legal, and political.

Furthermore, ethical questions are involved here that are cheapened or ignored by being dismissed as "puritanical" ravings. Here I have in mind the ill use of a secretary, friends, cabinet members, loyal supporters, even the President's spouse — all brought into an orbit of deceit and cover-up, perhaps even criminal wrongdoing in the securing of a job for the "woman in question" in exchange for her silence in a lawsuit. How can this possibly be construed as merely private and thus off limits to public deliberation, debate, and judgment?

Here it is important to remember that the President of the United States is more than a company head. The CEO model that many of the President's defenders have been pressing on us is unworthy of a democratic nation and will not work, not unless one believes that our civic life comes down to what the stock market is doing. The office of President — I repeat, the *office* of President — is a complex and even harrowing one that historically involves or presupposes a kind of affective bond between a President and the American people. Once a President is elected, he is *our* President. We may not have voted for him, but if he occupies the White House, then he is ours. We are called upon to respond to his appeals, especially when he commits American blood and treasure in times of war and crisis.

But even those who do not agree with his policies must assume a level of integrity and decency on a President's part. He is part of our lives for at least four years. Presidents pronounce on everything from the status of the Russian ruble to school safety, from balancing budgets to how to get more balanced meals for poor children. If — as the American people have concluded — the president is of low moral character and his word cannot be trusted, then he cannot do his job effectively. If everything the President says is subject to ridicule and reinterpretation because he has become untrustworthy, it becomes difficult, if not impossible, for him to govern effectively. He may last out a term, but he has become a place-holder, no longer a serious leader. Further, if we believe a President has behaved dishonorably and may even have broken the law (but that's okay because the subject is one "everybody" lies about), and we also claim that he is an "effective" leader nonetheless, then we have moved into a zone of amoral Machiavellianism that ill befits us as a people and that undermines a political system in which law has always been construed as more than a prohibitive or penal exercise. Rather, the law, ideally, embodies what is best, most capacious, and most hopeful about us as a people.

Where do these reflections lead us? Not to any knockdown answer

14

about what should be done. But, minimally, the implication is clear: these are serious matters that should be discussed seriously. The President is not "just our Bill." Remember the office. This is where the politics of forgiveness enters. There is something suspect about a dynamic of forgiveness-seeking that takes place only *after* various forms of polling and public opinion monitoring have gone forward to determine how this strategy will "play" with the public. There is something suspect about a dynamic of forgiveness-seeking that takes place with all the cameras rolling and a group of pastors as a kind of supporting cast to a confession. There is something suspect about a dynamic of forgiveness-seeking that presupposes, once the confession of being a sinner is made, and it is acknowledged (in the passive tense) that mistakes have been made and people have been hurt, that it can then move to legal and political exculpation as the endgame.

Something is radically wrong and troubling about this scenario. And it has nothing to do with demanding moral perfection of our leaders. All have sinned and fallen short. Few of us would want our lives examined with a fine-toothed comb and the results of that examination made public. At the same time, it is deadly to a decent democratic process to abandon altogether standards of minimally decent, honorable, and law-abiding behavior in our public figures.

We are a compassionate people at our best. We understand that justice must be tempered with mercy. But we cannot take leave of our senses and abandon judgment and deliberation altogether in the interest of sweeping a mess under the rug. The issue in this debate at this time, where forgiveness is concerned, involves the President of the United States. Kenneth Starr has not gone before ministers of God and sought absolution. Nor has any of the other players in this sordid psychodrama. But the President has, and that is why his behavior must be scrutinized critically by those charged with particular responsibility for evaluating the role of religion in public life, and public life in light of religion. Presumably, the results of that critical assessment would be applicable to any officeholder whose task it is to see that the laws are faithfully upheld.

Most of us are not under such a requirement as a feature of our office. Those who undertake public office have special responsibilities. They are neither below nor above the law. But we rightly care, or at least we used to, more about what they do *under cover of their office* than what the clerk in the department store does, or the traffic cop or the farmer.

Why? Because they have accepted and are charged with particular, clear responsibilities not incumbent upon the rest of us. We all have a duty to follow the law, unless it is blatantly unjust. But not all of us have a duty to uphold it. This point has been altogether eclipsed in the current debate, and it signals very troubling trends when forgiveness is played out as a political strategy. That strategy is tethered to the notion that if the person who sinned — and the President has described himself in this way — is sincere and really trying to put things right, then the writ of the law ceases to run and the process of public deliberation comes to a dead halt, including whether or not we expect Presidents in our time to treat all women as persons of dignity rather than to treat some women as means to a rather low and reckless end.[2]

I have been saddened by the reemergence of old-fashioned sexism in the public debate: "she snapped her thong"; "she was stalking him"; "he's a guy and all guys lie about sex." Is this how far we have come in the relations between the sexes? Or, rather, is this how low we think we should go to exonerate the President and remove from his shoulders any responsibility for his actions? One can seek forgiveness, struggle and grapple with one's deeds, work to mend broken relationships, strive to restore depleted trust and confidence, and at the same time recognize that there may well be public penalties that remain for one's behavior.

If we do not move in this direction, then we are stuck in the moral twilight zone exemplified in a column that appeared shortly before Thanksgiving Day, 1998, in our "national newspaper," sad as that may be, *USA Today*. The columnist notes polls showing that the American people are "eager to forgive President Clinton," and he links this to our "New Testament" founding ("clemency and grace") by contrast to the "Old Testament judgment of an 'eye for an eye.'"[3] The columnist then

---

2. Remember the phrase "that woman. . . ." Any woman, unless she has her head resolutely stuck in the sand, understands the meaning of that locution.

3. To call this a gross distortion of the Hebrew tradition is to understate. But here is an example — but one among thousands — of what passes for *popular* wisdom today. And it is that popular wisdom I am challenging because it is precisely what the President and his handlers are playing to and relying on. The "Op-Ed" in question is Armstrong Williams, "Clinton Case Highlights National Trait of Mercy," *USA Today* (Nov. 23, 1998, p. 23A). Williams also notes the outpouring of clemency appeals in behalf of Karla Faye Tucker before her execution in Texas. But this example, tucked in amidst the others, shows what happens when moral leveling proceeds apace. Nobody asked that Tucker be let out of jail

16

points to other moments of our gracious "clemency," including toward O. J. Simpson, whose post-trial support has been "remarkable" considering the nature of the double homicide charges against him. He even points to the behavior of the Dallas Cowboys, who, despite "drug charges and accusations of other crimes . . . remain the nation's most popular football team." It is the "Cowboys' winning spirit" that "captures hearts," and thus people are prepared to forgive their bad behavior even if they do not "condone" it.

Is this where we have arrived as a culture? Shouldn't our public leaders work to counter this sort of antinomianism rather than play to it? Personal sincerity is *not* the issue. The role of forgiveness and the use or abuse of that role for political ends is. I do not doubt the President's torment over his behavior. I do, however, most respectfully challenge the misuse of forgiveness for narrow political ends and purposes, whoever the President may be and whatever he may stand for. This is a sorry moment in our national life.

---

for her crimes. The question was whether, in light of her in-prison transformation, attested to by all concerned, the death penalty was an appropriate penalty. There *was* penalty: the question was which sort. And, of course, as everyone knows, our founding was explicitly constitutional — laws and duties — and not foundationally denominational. But this moves into the whole complex story of religion and American life and history more generally, and I cannot address it in this short piece.

Broken Covenants:
A Threat to Society?

MAX L. STACKHOUSE

I signed this Declaration for one simple reason. I agree with its contention that more is at stake in the current debates about Clinton than his sexual behavior with an intern, which I think is tawdry, and his avowed social policies, with which I mostly agree. Further, I disagree with those who have refused to offer public criticism of his behavior because they think it may further disrupt the programs that they want him to advance or may give comfort to his political enemies. It is less the actions of the President, which might have been predicted from reports of previous patterns of behavior, than the winking at or justifications of his behavior by the cultured opinion makers of press, academia, and pulpit that are the peril to society in the long run. It is, quite possibly, a betrayal of the office of the public intellectual — and especially of a public theologian — to adjust judgments according to short-term political effects. That may be the task of the hired "spin doctor" responding to hot news releases, but it is not the task of those professionals who must identify, clarify, and enhance the deeper structures of justice in and for our common life when things are messy.

Still, I must admit that I agonized about signing the Declaration for two reasons. First, I am not sure what to make of President Clinton's public confession of sin at the Prayer Breakfast and his letter to his church. I know that some signers suspect that these are no more than politically calculated acts, and I suspect that they may be right. But if

18

these actions are not a sham display, they could be genuine expressions of contrition simply offered in a form and style that this Yankee Democrat and Congregationalist finds unseemly but not necessarily inauthentic. I leave the discerning of the heart of Clinton's intent to God and the analysis of the dynamics of contrition and forgiveness to my colleagues.

In alliance with them, however, I am finally more concerned with the widespread neglect of fundamental issues about the character and direction of our society among those who are too quick to overlook what appear to be the President's violations of public covenants. I intentionally refer to the biblical, theological, and sociopolitical term that Clinton used in his first campaign for president, then unaccountably abandoned, leaving the door open to a resurgence of mere "contractual" moral thinking on many fronts. It is not moralism that is at stake here but the question of the basic ethical shape of our society, which his actions, its consequences, and his defenders appear to have eroded.

The second reason I hesitated was this: I did not want to see this Declaration used as a tool to legitimate the Special Investigator's or the Congress's handling of this matter, in some ways as tawdry as what was revealed to the public about Clinton's affairs and possibly also a betrayal of public trust. Thus, I was pleased when we decided to release the statement after the election. It is not a political document in the immediate and partisan sense, although it is obviously driven by a theologically based and ethically focused concern for civil society, and thus it is political in the deeper, wider, longer, if indirect, public theological sense. This may need some explanation.

The term "public theology," of course, is in dispute and has taken several forms. Not a few advocates simply intend it as going public with position statements that are derived from this or that religious preference. Surely it is true that if everyone joins public debates from some ideological or interested point of view, and all are free to do so in our system, religious voices must be as free to advance their views in the marketplace of ideas without apology as are those who hold to this or that economic, cultural, or philosophical dogma. But that is not my point.

The more profound forms of public theology have a rather refined sense of what theology is about and a pluralistic, social view of what the core of public life is. *Theology*, in this view, may be based in some way on an attempt to set forth a highly particular faith in a more

19

or less coherent fashion. But one of its tasks is to clarify a comprehending frame of reference (only by including God in the purview of reasonable discourse could anything be comprehending) by which the moral and spiritual architecture of the common life, including national politics, can be understood and ultimately guided. If Muslims or Hindus or Christians of this or that stripe (Catholics or Evangelicals or Calvinists, for example) speak to public issues, they must make a plausible case that their view of God and logical discourse is pertinent and adequate to the issues.

And the "public" implied in this view of the common life refers not in the first instance to government or political action but to the prior, pluriform arena of social relationships formed by networks of dedicated persons who sustain the institutions, organizations, associations, advocacy groups, and especially religious communities that form, articulate, and actualize an ethos in which human civility may flourish. It is the families, churches, schools, businesses, lodges, service clubs, neighborhood improvement associations, cultural advancement organizations, charitable institutions, corporations, unions, hospitals, colleges, minority advancement associations, community orchestras, sports clubs, mutual aid societies, support groups, advocacy movements, and political parties that constitute civil society. It is a matter of historical record that most of these have deep roots in communities of faith; and religious ethics continues to evoke the personal commitment to get involved and to actualize the deep values that form public life over time. Government, in this view, is the servant of this public complex — neither its author nor its master.

This larger view has within it an implicit criticism of a widespread view of public life in the United States. Some readings of American life have adopted a "two agent" theory of public life. One agent is, of course, individuals ideally (sadly, not always actually) honoring each other irrespective of race, gender, class, religion, or national origin. The other agent is governmental states, nations (foreign and native-American), or branches thereof, the loci of legitimate authority. One of the benefits of this view is that, in principle, it respects the human rights of each and provides structures of law for the protection of persons. But a two-agent view also allows us to lurch from rampant, libertarian individualism in the name of freedom in some areas of life to a bureaucratic statism in the name of progressive responsibility for the common good in other areas. Public theology, in contrast, is opposed to the militant Republican view supported by some on "the Christian Right" who would dismantle government in the name of individual freedom, and to the left-Democratic view supported by some "Socialist Christians," who propose more and bigger government to address every human need. The "New Democratic" movement that brought Clinton to power, like the recent ouster of Speaker Gingrich on the part of the Republicans, can be seen as an attempt to dismantle the extremes to which the two-agent view can lead.

The problem with this two-agent view is that it fails to account for, protect, or nurture what is actually the core of public life: the rich array of mediating institutions, voluntary associations, and intervening organizations that stand between the individual and the government in a society. This is the view that not only is it is a free country and some freedoms must be protected and ordered by law, but that all have a duty to ask, "What kinds of communities should we form and sustain to make life better for all?" The generation of self-governing, creative organizations is the glory of the American public legacy, as the Puritan colonialists knew, as the authors of the Bill of Rights demanded, as Alexis de Tocqueville recognized, and as those who civilized the frontier, fought against slavery, fascism, and communism, and struggled for civil rights showed. It is our most precious gift to the world.

This more excellent view accents the fact that all persons are, whether we know it or not, called to participate in communities of responsibility that stand under a moral law and, for divine purposes, that transcend every person and all political orders. It has a richer view of public life, and it knows and cultivates a network of groupings that populate and animate the moral space between self and collectivity, which we call "civil society." This is the incarnate center of moral capital, the locus of the measure of social grace, justice, and peace possible in history.

To be sure, the two-agent theory allows persons to make voluntary agreements and form contracts, but the relationships people form on that basis may quickly be dissolved if they are not immediately satisfying. No enduring duty or right, no sustained friendship to share responsibility for the common good, and no formation of or accountability for behavior with regard to ongoing communities of commitment are required. In such an environment, the personal is decidedly not political; the sharpest of lines may be drawn between "private" and "public," and no one is accountable for "low crimes and misdemeanors" as long as they are voluntary and between adults.

21

This framework is not only superficial but pernicious. The private "individual" is not the whole self. The soul of a person is not fulfilled by claiming its sovereign autonomy any more than it is by being swallowed in some governmental whole. Rather, it is most deeply discovered by being in a wholesome relationship with God and the neighbor. People actually live in multiple relationships of personal life, and flourish best when they live in responsible ones marked by committed reciprocity, enduring mutuality, and behavioral boundaries. Nor is the nation enhanced by a view that sees it as the most comprehending "public." It ever stands under the righteousness of God and is but one of the communities for whom God cares. To think of the common good only nationally is neither common enough nor good enough — something we should easily recognize in a global era. Besides, regimes rise and fall, whereas the inner moral architecture of a civilization, inevitably shaped by deep and long-term religious influences, both endures as rulers pass and overlaps with other peoples and places. That moral architecture is only sustained by the active communities of society and is only made effective by the kind of leadership that builds up the moral and spiritual fabric of these communities. It is a tragic error to understand human persons, social reality, ethics, or political life in terms of the two agencies of private individual and public government, especially if we neglect the religious and theological factors that are decisive for them both.

Two great traditions of public theology have developed highly suggestive ways of treating the fabric of social life and giving it moral guidance. One, most clearly articulated by the Roman Catholic tradition in the West but present in other traditions also, can be referred to by the term "subsidiarity." This is the view that God wants us to live in an organically based and sacramentally confirmed set of hierarchically arranged relationships, some closer to the grass roots of everyday life and others at higher levels of authority. In this view, all who hold higher office, political or ecclesiastical, should honor and support those institutions at the base, for example, families, parishes, schools, and hospitals, and see that these are strengthened in every moral, spiritual, and material way. Behaviors that threaten or violate them are to be brought under judgment.

The second great tradition of public theology argues for a more horizontal series of bodies or organizations in society. In this view, the good society is one in which dedicated persons actively participate in a series of covenanted associations, with representatives of the pluralistic parts gathering periodically to discern what is just and loving if some behavior violates one or several of the covenants that hold society together. Most often advocated by those traditions deriving from the Reformation, but present elsewhere also, this view holds that the biblical idea of covenant not only rightly portrays God's relationship to the faithful but is the model for responsible participation in all the federated spheres of social life. Each area of life is to live under God's law, for Godly ends, and with due attention to the particular callings of life. In this view, the calling of political leadership is both to administer the agencies of state and to lead a party and the nation by word and example in such a way that the government protects and fosters the ongoing vitality of the covenanted spheres in a federated civil society.

While these two forms of public theology may disagree about hierarchy and federalism, neither the classic hierarchical-subsidiary or federal-covenantal views want to establish a church-dominated politics. But the public theologies of these traditions do demand the acknowledgment of the indispensable moral and spiritual aspects of the institutions of civil society and the fact that these are ethically and socially prior to politics. Thus they demand that political leaders, if they are to keep the loyalty of the people, attract the best minds in the several fields of social analysis and leadership; that they claim the moral legitimacy that religious authorities can offer or withhold; that they must respect, protect, and enhance the core associations and communities of the common life. Thus they treat with grave seriousness threats to the tissues of social life or the betrayal of the bonds whereby the various primal communities of life are sustained, since in this way the foundations of civil society are undercut and the long-term viability of public life is damaged.

With our basic stance regarding social ethics in view, we come to the crux of these matters as they bear on assessing the actions of President Clinton. Did he or did he not violate the covenant of marriage and the sacred vows he took with Hillary before God and the civil law? The fact that others, including other presidents (not to mention King David long ago), a great number of kings and queens, members of Congress, leading academics, Protestant clergy, foreign statesmen, and moral leaders such as Gandhi and Martin Luther King, Jr., might also have done so is irrelevant. Today, in our present context, where people deny the connection between the capacity to keep marital covenants and the capacity to keep covenants that are decisive for professional and public life, it is being argued not only that people have made grave mistakes but that these mistakes are morally and socially irrelevant. In fact, the grave mistakes of others are often hidden precisely because people in other times and places recognized that such errors of judgment and behavior do, in fact, affect the public good, the capacity of leaders to claim a moral legitimacy for the policies they advocate, and the well-being of public life itself. In addition, the evidence mounts that the crisis of family life in our civil society is a very serious hidden time bomb, only partly exposed by ingenuous rhetoric about "family values," and not yet widely acknowledged by academics and clergy who passively accept or overtly celebrate those forms of sexual liberation that erode family stability. There is a long-term social price to pay that cannot be avoided. It is morally and intellectually dishonest to deny it or to relegate the issue to oblivion.

We can also ask whether President Clinton did or did not violate his pledge before God and the people to uphold the Constitution of the United States when he lied in a legal deposition in a civil court suit. If we argue that it is common for people to do so, and that this level of procedure is not really legally serious, then we have agreed either that the President has sworn to uphold a law that is unjust — and thus not to be obeyed — or that the President is not subject to a just law. There is little evidence that this experience prompted him to seek a reform of an unjust law, one that, in fact, influences the daily life of many people and, for some, the destiny of their lives and that of their children. The fact that thousands have had to fudge the facts in order to avoid being devastated by low-level justice, which is where most people run into the court system, is a scandal in a civil society, and few public intellectuals, let alone theologians, are addressing these issues.

Another area that needs inquiry regards President Clinton's treatment of his closest advisors and members of his cabinet. No political leader of a complex society can dream of governing without a cadre of trusted and trusting talent that dedicates a major segment of their lives to serving a grand purpose, often at personal and financial sacrifice. These are people who give much to nurture those sectors of society that need protection and care from the government — labor, commerce, state, education, health and human services, the interior, and so forth. It is evident that Clinton lied to and used his closest friends, advisors, and supporters from these areas. They trusted him and identified with the priorities he wanted to make effective. He broke the covenants of friendship in the deep political sense of the indispensable network of advisors and confidants of extraordinary competence who were capable of developing and carrying out a (mostly) coherent vision of and for the nation. In this regard, Clinton also deceived his devoted followers in the leadership of the Democratic party. The long-range ramifications are not yet visible, but the number and quality of those who have been quietly resigning from their posts in the cabinet, staff, or party and turning to other ventures in society are more telling than has been revealed.

A more complex question is whether Clinton has kept faith with the African-American community, with which, for which, and from which great empathy for him is visible. In some ways that community remains a major bellwether of the moral health of civil society, given its history of slavery and segregation. History will judge us by how this segment of society fares. The issues were already clear in the President's 1993 address to the Convocation of the Church of God in Christ, a black denomination, when the debates about health care and welfare reform were in full swing. Taking them as advocates for a number of ethnic and poverty communities in relative social crisis, he said, "Where there are no families, where there is no order, where there is no hope, where we are reducing the size of the military because we have won the Cold War, who will be there to give structure, discipline and love to children? You [the clergy] must do that and we [the government] must help."[1]

What seems to be clear is that the clergy, especially the black and Hispanic clergy, have sought to assume the challenge. The development of parachurch organizations to help the disadvantaged has grown enormously. They seek to mend broken families, to reclaim bitter and dispirited youth, to aid the needy who are unemployable, to tutor those who are employable but without the social skills for the job world, and to generate local businesses and employment. Many have begun day-care and after-school programs, and a few have formed independent schools. But it is not clear that the churches and their spin-off service organizations can do everything. As health care has devolved increasingly to the HMO's and welfare to the states and cities, the evidence is slim that the President has enabled the government to aid these activi-

---

1. *New York Times* (November 14, 1993, p. 24).

ties. It is surely so, as he said, that "the days of big government are over"; but society needs a political and social vision concerning how we might best help the neighbor in need under new conditions, and we are not getting that. Few today want to return to the old health-care and welfare systems. But the political leadership required to make the evolving systems more just, compassionate, and effective has been so distracted by successive scandals that those who want to help do not know where to turn, even if they oppose Clinton's opponents more.

On other levels, in the midst of the crises over his sexual escapades, the President went first to Africa and later to China, and he made appearances in attempts to bring a stable peace to Israel and to Ireland. He was greatly honored in all these settings. Further, he has made speeches about the difficult situations in Russia, the Balkans, and Brazil. In each place, he has (in my view) said exactly the right things. But, having said what needed to be said, there is little evidence that he has followed up on the most important points. The deeper reconstruction of the covenants of civil society that could assure greater commitment to development in Africa, human rights in China, and a more stable peace in several regions is not entirely in the President's hands, of course. But a preoccupation with the ambiguities in his own life has made the transition from good insight to operational reality difficult. It is a false view of social and political life today to expect that they could be isolated.

I do not know whether the President will be or should be impeached for these things. That is for the members of Congress to decide, and it may be that some political deal will be worked out that will cause the least damage to society and avoid the embarrassments that prolonged hearings would entail for a gifted politician, a great party, and a nation struggling to be a responsible member of a now-global society. But in terms of the public theologies of subsidiarity and covenant, the best models we have of how God wants us to live as public community, it is very difficult to say that we should simply get past this and return to an agenda of the equivalents of the New Deal, the Great Society, or the War on Poverty.

We may have to acknowledge that we do not have, or deserve, a great statesman in our time. We may pray that we can find a responsible way to reconstruct our languishing civil society below the state and contribute to the formation of a global civil society beyond it, so that we can become more of a blessing than a curse to humanity. It will take every shred of moral insight and spiritual energy that can be marshaled to overcome the long-run disabilities into which Clinton and his defenders have led us. On the deeper ethical and social levels, that is difficult to forgive.

Why Clinton Is
Incapable of Lying:
A Christian Analysis

STANLEY HAUERWAS

You cannot help but wonder who President Clinton is. What a licking
he has taken but, like the proverbial watch, he keeps on ticking. You
would think he would like to slink off to the desert for some serious soul
searching, but he seems not to have considered that an option. I suspect
that is not an option because he assumes that his current embarrassment is but "more politics." For Bill Clinton, moreover, it is politics all
the way down.

I think it worth speculating about President Clinton's character
because I fear that the current concerns about his "private life" and
subsequent lying to the country are not anomalous given the character
of the modern politician. Bill Clinton is what we should expect, given
our politics. In short, I fear that for some time the people America has
been producing to run our bureaucracies (whether those bureaucracies
are "public" or "private") do not have souls sufficient to make them li-
ars. To be a liar is a considerable moral achievement because the lie at
least must pay homage to some notion of the truth. I suspect that our
politics no longer presumes to be about truth in any shape or form, and
thus we get the politicians we deserve.

How could anyone go through a campaign for President and still
pretend to be a truth teller? There are so many different groups to

which one must appeal. I sometimes think that our elections are analogous to the practices of some South Sea people, who first degrade a candidate for king before crowning him the new king. They put the candidate in a cage, taunt him unmercifully, make him eat garbage, defecate on him, and finally take him from cage to crown and worship him. Our elections are meant to ensure that anyone we elect to public office has lost his or her hold on the truth. It is all a matter of "spin." Moreover, I do not think that this is a recent development; rather, it is part and parcel of the American political system. If you doubt that, I ask you to reread Henry Adams's wonderful novel *Democracy*.

Clinton, I suspect, understands and has accepted this system from the beginning. He feels no need to go to the desert and repent because, when all is said and done, it is just politics. To describe Clinton as an opportunist is not, therefore, interesting. What politician or — to change the context — ambitious academic is not? Most people who want to be "dean" in the modern academy do so not because they want to do anything but because they want to be dean. Most of those who want to be president of this or that do so for the same reason. They now have an office, which means you must regard them but they do not necessarily have to regard you.

In fact, I think Clinton did want to do something. If Clinton cares about anything, he cares about furthering civil rights. For that he is to be commended. The civil rights movement is for Clinton, as well as for many of his generation, his church. To be for freedom and equality of opportunity for African-Americans has given these people a sense that their life has a moral compass. Everything else is "private." The problem, of course, is that the civil rights agenda does not supply the moral skills to determine how one ought to live out "the private." In that sphere (the sphere of "the private") all that matters is that whatever you do and whatever you do with someone else ought to be done "freely," that is, with consent. So you can do whatever you want to do as long as you do not harm anyone else "too much."

I am sure President Clinton is very sorry he got caught. Indeed, I suspect that at least one of the reasons he lied to the country about his affair with Monica was that he did not want to hurt his wife or daughter. His lie, therefore, is an indication that he is not entirely without a soul. There is, of course, no way we can know the complex relations represented by his family; but one assumes that he tells himself he is doing such important work, moral work, as President that he can indulge privately as long as no one gets hurt. That is why the problem from his perspective is not what he did, but that he got caught. The problem was not a little sex with someone other than one's wife. That is but another "relationship." Rather, from his perspective his "sin" was stupidity.

Given this analysis, saying that his confession at the Presidential Prayer Breakfast was insincere or cynical is an inadequate account of the challenge before us. Indeed, I suspect that Clinton was as sincere as he could be. Indeed, I suspect he is "truly religious," given that his religion is the civil religion represented in the churches of mainstream Protestantism. He assumes that religion is supposed to have something to do with the "inner life"; and he assumes that his "problem" needs to be handled through sessions of "pastoral counseling" because he is a "liberal Baptist" who has been taught that religious faith is supposed to give one's life "meaning." Thus "pastoral counseling" supplies the psychologized religious technologies to free him from his "sexual addiction." One cannot help but wonder whether some of those involved in counseling Clinton would be so involved if Clinton's politics were those of Ronald Reagan.

It is not just that President Clinton has no sense that a public sin requires public penance — for example, standing barefoot in the snow — but that American Protestantism has no sense of it either. Why should we expect President Clinton to have any sense of the public harm his sin has done when he has seen no form of Christian practice that would suggest that sin is an offense against God and the church? His generalized "confession" to a "generalized" god and community are but the mirror image of the generalized confessions of sin into which most Christians are schooled in church. Moreover, we are schooled by such a confessional practice because a truthful practice of confession, repentance, and reconciliation would entail that the church become a disciplined community at odds with the politics that produced Bill Clinton.

For example, did anyone at First Baptist Church in Little Rock ever suggest to Bill Clinton that he ought to think twice about going into politics? Did anyone test him about his "ambition" to see whether such an ambition was what the church discerned was the best use of his talents? Did anyone ever say to Bill Clinton that if he chose to run for office, he would be tempted to say less than the truth, but since he was a baptized member of First Baptist Church of Little Rock, he would be expected to tell the truth? Did anyone at First Baptist Church of Little

Rock say that if he lost an election for telling the truth, they would not abandon him as a brother in Christ? How would Bill Clinton, in the absence of such a community, have ever known that even going into politics might be a way to put his salvation in jeopardy?

Therefore, I fear that when the Declaration urges the society to take up the ethical commitments necessary for a civil society to seek the integrity of both public and private morality, we only reinforce a distinction that has created the problem. If the above questions had been forced on Bill Clinton at the First Baptist Church of Little Rock, the church would have been "violating his privacy." But that is what I am suggesting we must recover if Christians are to serve in the kind of politics that we call democracy. For what we have to give to such a politics is people who have learned as part of their baptisms not only to tell the truth but to *be* the truth. Such people have no use for abstract distinctions between the private and the public because they know their lives are not their own.

I am aware that Christians schooled by the "realism" of Reinhold Niebuhr may find such a demand too "demanding," particularly when applied to the "wider political society." But if such people of truth do not exist, then the "wider political society" will be even more a desert. Bill Clinton is in a desert, but he has no way of knowing that because he has long ago been abandoned by any church that could help him discover what kind of life he had taken up.

I confess that I am not particularly concerned whether Bill Clinton is or is not impeached. Rather, I pray that we might discover as Christians how to be a church that is capable of speaking the truth in a politics that produces people like Bill Clinton. The question before Christians is not whether Bill Clinton should be impeached, but why he is not excommunicated.

President Clinton and the Privatization of Morality

FR. MATTHEW L. LAMB

There is a great paradox in American culture. On the one hand, society exalts the individual as free and autonomous, while, on the other hand, that autonomous and free individual is not really respected in his or her concrete existence, with all the dramatic choices he or she makes and actions he or she performs. The individual becomes a subject of conversation — a specimen for the talk shows — rather than a freely responsible agent who must take responsibility for his or her decisions. This happens because those supposedly free choices are not respected as either conforming to, or being opposed to, the orientation of human freedom toward the truly good. When we privatize morality, rather than really promoting personal responsibility and individuality, we empty the decisions and actions that are most uniquely our own, that make us into the persons we are, of any public moral relevance. Instead of moral argument in public, there is only a procedural role-playing. A mask or public persona can take on a range of roles without ever revealing who the person behind the mask really is. We can, as Nietzsche remarked, forget who we really are as we excel now in this job, now in that role.

This is dramatized poignantly in the scandals associated with President Clinton. The polls chart a presidential job approval with an indifference to the President's failure to take full and public responsibility for his very public deceptions. Infidelity is deemed a private matter that casts its mantle of privacy over very public deception and perjury about it. Not surprisingly, President Clinton has appealed to that other "private sphere" of our American life, religion, to further isolate his public deceptions from public judgment. The privatizing of morality follows upon the privatizing of religion. The exclusion of religion from public discussions of the good, which accompanied the privatization of religion, ends by divorcing morality from public conduct. President Clinton's deceptions represent another step in a journey American culture has been on for some time: the privatization of not only religion but also morality. If there is a church or synagogue or mosque somewhere off the public square, it is only there for the private consolation of those citizens who need some religion in their civil and commercial lives. Politicians and other public figures who wish to duck into them to escape taking full public responsibility for their illegal and/or immoral actions also find them useful.

The consequences of privatizing morality are far more severe than any public sanctions a Congress or Senate could impose. When human freedom is severed from judgments about the truly good, freedom loses its objective and public moorings. Questions about the good are the most public of all matters. To privatize such questions erodes any sense of the common good in society. In place of public arguments and judgments about the truly good, one substitutes a political enactment of laws and programs that are supposed to function even if the citizens themselves are not moral. Society does not need just citizens; it only needs technically and legally implemented programs and laws that function so well that, as Kant remarks, even a society of devils would agree with them. Politicians need only appear to be virtuous when it suits their manipulation of public opinion to maintain their power. So the defenders of the President point to his programs as being more important than whatever vices he may have. They point to laws and programs he promotes for health care, education, and the environment. These are taken as more important moral or justice imperatives than any conduct. Michael Sandel has analyzed this instrumentalization of public discourse and practice as procedural liberalism.

The American privatization of morality is rooted in a twofold abandonment. Gone is the classical insistence on a genuinely public need for moral and intellectual virtues on the part of citizens and politicians. Gone as well is a Jewish and Christian insistence on the theological virtues of faith, hope, and charity informing and strengthening those moral and intellectual virtues in the face of evil and widespread injustice.

In place of a colorful and rich pluralism with serious and profound arguments about what is truly good for the body politic, there results a drab and mechanical indifferentism, with polls and votes driven by commercials and mass manipulation. With no objective norms for human freedom, conscience becomes totally privatized. Each individual is free to choose whatever he or she pleases. Freedom is defined as an *indifference* or neutrality toward choice-worthy human ends. Human rights become codes of sovereignty and power, trumping any notion of human nature. Democracy declines into merely procedural nose-counting as elections are driven not by spirited and substantive public debates on what is truly good for the society but by money, mass commercials, and polls. Elections decline into exactly what journalists call them: horse races.

As a Roman Catholic theologian I leave to others to discuss whether or not President Clinton has repented and been forgiven according to the norms of his Baptist faith and theology. Catholic theology would indicate that, besides personal repentance and confessional forgiveness, there are public moral implications of the very public scandal that the President gave. The sin of scandal occurs when one directly induces another to commit sin either materially or formally, for example, by soliciting a person to perjury, or to sins of the flesh, even if the person induced to this act is habitually or at the time disposed to commit it. The office of the Presidency, with its public representative character and manifold responsibilities, only adds to the gravity of the scandal. In such cases, whoever repents truly is obligated to attend to the mending of the public scandal he or she has caused. Personal repentance should never be abused as a way of dodging the just requirements of public reparation for public scandal.

As morality is privatized, scandal sounds quaint. Following the pattern of Catholic social teachings, recent encyclicals of Pope John Paul II on "The Splendor of Truth," "The Gospel of Life," and "Faith and Reason" seek to bring the intellectual, moral, and theological traditions of Catholicism to bear upon contemporary questions of morality and truth. Those traditions, drawing from the philosophies of ancient Greece and Rome, as well as from the traditions of Judaism and Islam in the patristic and medieval periods, contain achievements of wisdom and insight often rejected and forgotten in our modern and postmodern cultures. In this the Pope is calling attention to the personal and public importance of intellectual, moral, and theological virtues. The growing interest in what is sometimes referred to as virtue ethics is also seeking to recover these forgotten or ignored traditions.

Because a question or insight is ancient does not mean it is irrelevant for our time. Indeed, the Pope indicates how basic human questions are found in different ways in all cultures and times. Engaging those questions, and finding historic answers to them, may be just what we need to advance the genuine achievements of modernity and postmodernity. With these questions, memory becomes an exercise in much-needed wisdom. For example, cutting-edge advances today often demand inter- and cross-disciplinary collaboration in science, technology, and industry. Specialization is pressing for patterns of integration — an ancient task of wisdom. Wisdom aims at cultivating a heuristic knowledge and appreciation of wholes, and how parts are integrated within them. Think of the great concerns of environmental policies and sciences today.

The very public questions about the truly good are similar exercises in wisdom. Without them, modernity and postmodernity promote views of reality primarily constituted by individual matters with no overarching natural, God-given order. All groupings or associations of individuals become arbitrary, random, or conventional. The state or nation is primarily an extrinsic aggregate, constructed by the conventions of "social contracts." Morality is subordinated to conventional legality. An ethic of friendship, justice, and virtue is replaced by an ethic of Kantian duty or utilitarian law. Against modern and postmodern conventionalism, Catholic intellectual traditions witness to premodern understandings of natural law, of human beings as essentially social, and of society itself as organic and cooperative. Such Catholic, as well as other premodern philosophical and religious, traditions offer much for a needed transformation of modern and postmodern contexts of industrialized and information societies with complex global exchange economies.

Catholic moral teachings, whether dealing with social or with sexual questions, seek to promote an attentiveness to the ways in which the universal is grasped in the concrete and particular. Far from being an impoverished conceptual universal, as with Hegel, or a voluntaristic categorical imperative, as with Kant, Catholic wisdom draws human attention to how the morally good is the truly good, and so always calls for attentive attunement to reality as created and redeemed by God in Christ Jesus. Such attunement recognizes that the intelligibility and responsibility of acting persons is precisely in how their experiences, meanings, and values are either truly good or not. Truth can never be simply private; it is also always public. As Plato and Aristotle indicated, and the Greek and Latin fathers insisted even more strongly, truth is infinitely shareable. Truth does not depend on honor or wealth or public opinion. Truth transcends all these. Christian faith knows that truth is ultimately interpersonal: Jesus Christ with the Father and the Holy Spirit. Even though only Jesus, his mother, and the small band of his disciples proclaimed in word and deed the kingdom of God, his truth transcended all the might and wealth and power of the Roman Empire, and will continue to transcend all earthly power, wealth, and might.

As the Pope remarks, we Christians must repent of the many ways in which we have substituted coercive force for the truth, betraying the cross by the sword. It was the European wars of religion that led the founders of modernity to mistake power for truth, and so construct social contracts that abandoned wisdom and virtue for power and law. Physical and social reality was misconstrued as nothing but fields of force; violence was misread into all of nature, including human nature. The Enlightenment thinkers linked their imagined state of nature with states of war. Individuals were fitted with the armor of certain "rights" with which they could engage in the never-ending battles for self-assertion.

Wisdom, on the contrary, sees persons in relation to many other persons. No one can narrate who he or she is without telling of his or her families, friends, loved ones. Only in relation to others is a human person assured of his or her own unique identity. Moreover, in Catholic teaching, only through virtue and choosing the good are individual persons genuinely attuned to others and able to expand their effective freedom. Vice and sin contract freedom and isolate the acting person from the self's own nature and from other human beings. This is at the basis of the privatization of morality.

This privatization leads to a nihilistic denial of particular individuals, especially the weakest and the voiceless. Thus it is hardly unrelated to the President's scandals that he is adamant in rejecting any legal limitations on the availability of abortions. In abortion decisions, the mother, the doctor, or the law arrogates the power to decide when a human being is human. There is a public indifference to the truly good and truly evil character of human choices and actions. What is fostered is a cancerous indifference to the developing fetus in the womb of the mother. Such indifference can never be confined to the unborn. Thus the Supreme Court's 1992 decision in *Planned Parenthood vs. Casey* provides a very privatized definition of freedom: "At the heart of liberty is the right to define one's own concept of existence, of meaning, of the universe, and of the mystery of human life." This then provides the premise for a decision in the U.S. District Court in the state of Washington in favor of a right to physician-assisted suicide. What the Pope calls a "culture of death" spreads its shadows over the land.

If each individual has a right to "define one's own concept of existence, of meaning, of the universe," certainly the President has the right to define his own concepts of "is," "sex," and "sexual relations." Already a few lawyers are appealing to "the Clinton defense" to provide their own concepts of "perjury" and "obstruction of justice." Congress is debating very diverse definitions of "high crimes and misdemeanors." The privatization of morality leads to the debasement of the language. In extremity each American would become a linguistic solipsist — a terrible instantiation of Leibniz's monads. Without proper attention to the truly good, the legal and court system will over time decline into a corrupt theater where money, power, and deception rob them of any semblance of justice.

In Catholic teaching, the "heart of liberty" is not a creatorlike right to come up with "one's own concept of existence, of meaning, of the universe, of the mystery of human life." At the heart of liberty is a natural orientation toward the good. When we choose evil, our freedom constricts, as the various forms of addiction in our society illustrate. For human freedom only expands when we choose the truly good in accord with God's created and redeemed order.

A nihilistic indifference spreads like a cancer that erodes the very fabric of family and social life. The real differences of concrete individuals lose their value. Marriage is seen as no more than an arbitrary social contract that is indifferent to the sex of the spouses and to children. Where natural family planning respects the individuality of each married couple, educates the couple's freedom in the virtues of moderation, and encourages the male to respect the natural rhythms of his wife's fertility, artificial birth control is totally indifferent to the contingent differences of each couple. It is a mechanical or biotechnological "quick fix" that severs the procreative act from its specifically human context of mutual love and trust. Many Latin Americans, Africans, and Asians warn against what they see as the "contraceptive and abortion imperialism" being promoted by the Clinton/Gore administration.

Freedom is reduced to nihilistic indifference, not a genuine choice of the good of the spouse. Prevalent divorce simply rejects the indissolubility of marriage — testifying to the indifference of one spouse or another. Increasing paternity and maternity outside of marriage spread an indifference to whether a child is conceived by one father or another, one mother or another. Similar to divorce, this has profoundly negative effects on the children. Indeed, contrary to Catholic teaching, birth is decisively cut off from its intrinsic natural orientation to the education of the child. Children, especially sons, do not know their fathers and the life education they give, form gangs, and plague our cities and towns — not unlike what happened in Europe during the so-called Dark Ages, when families broke down and cities declined into widespread anarchy. Historians of the family indicate how it took the Church about six centuries to rebuild the family by insisting that, no matter how rich or poor, marriage was the indissoluble union of husband and wife for a life dedicated to the procreation and education of children. The privatization of morality severs human rights from human nature and personal dignity. Human rights are often proclaimed in general terms, but then concrete and particular human beings are left to grapple with the free choices they are making — which will affect other concrete human beings. Indifferent abstractions of a secularist humanism replace concrete human beings making real decisions. "The more I love humanity in general, the less I love man in particular," the doctor confesses in Dostoyevsky's *The Brothers Karamazov*.

This indifference seeps into all facets of American life. Ironically, the much-vaunted individualism of people in the United States is in fact much less attentive to real individual differences than it claims. Individual, personal, and unique lives and friendships are far less cherished and cultivated than they should be. The United States of America and its many and diverse peoples deserve a far more organic, colorful, and humane pluralism than the drab indifference and uniform multiculturalist mall beyond good and evil. Both publicly and personally we should not be indifferent to the responsibility to truth each one of us faces in the exercise of his or her freedom. The scandals and deceptions of President Clinton are more deeply woven into the fabric of American life than many of us may wish to acknowledge. They illustrate — and unfortunately promote — the privatization of morality that endangers both the public and the personal lives of all of us.

Missing the Point on Clinton

DON S. BROWNING

Jim Wall's two recent editorials for the most part miss the point on the crisis surrounding Bill Clinton. He concentrates far too much on Clinton's philandering and almost ignores the larger legal and moral issues.

During late summer (Aug. 26 to Sept. 2), Wall argued that Clinton's apologies were not deep enough. After the White House [Religious Leaders'] Prayer Breakfast, however, he believes that Clinton had "more than made up for his less-than-contrite" earlier confession. Now Wall (Oct. 14) feels that the public humiliation of Clinton has been punishment enough. To do more is to border on reenacting the Salem witch trials and to allow the "fundamentalist," "right-wing," "puritanical" Ken Starr to win the day. Wall does not believe that there is a conspiracy, but there is a "pattern."

As a frequent contributor to the *Christian Century* and a liberal Democrat, I feel obligated to say that Wall's editorials are not providing the churches with the leadership on this issue that they deserve. Clinton has confessed only to sexual wrongdoing. But he is asking Congress and the American people to allow his limited confession and repentance of these acts to excuse him from the actual charges contained in the Starr referral — perjury, obstruction of justice, and abuse of presidential power.

Letter to the Editor, *The Christian Century*

Evidently, Wall believes that Clinton's sexual sins are so great that to confess to them covers all other misdeeds. In other words, if Clinton confesses to what he is not being charged with, he should be exonerated for all actual charges against him. It is as if one good confession ought to cover three or more additional wrongdoings. That would be a good return on his investment.

Wall believes that Starr was too vigorous in his methods, and that this gives Clinton the right to bend the truth before courts of law. Time will tell us whether this is true. But nothing Starr did forced Clinton not to tell the truth in his disposition on the Paula Jones case. If the Jones case was groundless, that is all the more reason for him to have been truthful. It should be equally clear that the details of Clinton's sexual relations are in the Starr referral because of Clinton's strained attempts to manipulate the court's legal definition of sex.

Impeachment may not be called for, but it makes a mockery of justice, the Presidency, and the price common people pay for such offenses if some form of official judgment, one way or the other, is not made. Hence, Congress must review the facts and make its decision. If Clinton is found guilty, then the remaining issue is this: are these high crimes and misdemeanors? And Congress is the rightful place for this decision as well. Wall's plea to call off the impeachment process makes too much of Clinton's sexual confessions and misses the actual issues at stake. We can forgive Clinton for his sexual wanderings, but unfortunately we must inquire into the rest, however much it diverts us from other important issues.

Dawdling toward Judgment: The Impeachment Issue and the Perennial Problems of Casuistry

JOHN LAWRENCE

The comprehensive ethical handbooks of the Jesuits are in part *monstra* of abomination and storehouses of execrable sins and filthy habits, the description and treatment of which provoke an outcry of disgust. The most shocking things are here dealt with in a brazen-faced way . . . not with the view of calling down with prophetic power . . . a heavier burden of judgment, but often enough with the view of representing the most disgraceful things as pardonable, and of showing to the most regardless transgressors a way in which they may still always obtain the peace of the Church.

Adolph von Harnack, *History of Dogma* (1889)[1]

jeremiad: a lamenting and denunciatory complaint; a doleful story; a dolorous tirade

Webster's Third New International Dictionary (1981)

1. Adolph von Harnack, *History of Dogma* (New York: Russell and Russell, 1958), VII, 101-2.

As the Clinton impeachment saga matured, we faced several paradoxes. The most surprising among them was a steadily rising public approval of the President's job performance. According to a long-term tracking poll conducted by *USA Today/CNN/GALLUP,* a mere 42 percent of its polling sample had approved of Clinton's job performance in the period January 5-7, 1996. This predated the Monica Lewinsky imbroglio by a full year. By October 9-12 of 1998, after the most thorough moral humiliation in the history of the American presidency, 65 percent of the polling sample approved "the way Bill Clinton is handling his job as president."[2] The more embarrassing and complete the revelations, the more resolutely the public has supported his continuation in office — even though they fully realize that the President has violated important moral and legal norms.[3] And by the time the impeachment process had officially begun, 74 percent of the *USA Today/CNN/Gallup* sample wanted the whole process to end, 39 percent of those without any kind of censure for the President.[4]

Why the disconnect between widely accepted ideals and public reluctance to impose official sanctions on Clinton for such egregious behavior? In part, I believe that we are seeing a kind of ethics fatigue in America. Responding to Watergate and Vietnam, legislators created a host of mandates and agencies empowered to define and to police ethics violations. Ethics investigations have become a routine of government. However, as Peter Morgan and Glenn Reynolds suggest in their book *The Appearance of Impropriety: How the Ethics Wars Have Undermined American Government, Business, and Society,*[5] Americans continued to experience declining confidence in government while they wit-

---

2. *USA Today/CNN/Gallup Poll* (October 19, 1998), www.cnn.com/archives/poll001.htm. The organization reports 1,004 members in its sampling group.

3. In another poll conducted by CNN/Gallup immediately after the airing of the President's video testimony before the Special Prosecutor's grand jury, a mere 28% thought that he was "telling the truth" and 56% thought that "he had perjured himself." Helen Kennedy, *New York Daily News* (September 23, 1998), Section News, 3.

4. *USA Today/CNN/Gallup Poll* (November 18, 1998) www.usatoday.com/news/poll001.htm.

5. Peter W. Morgan and Glenn H. Reynolds, *The Appearance of Impropriety: How the Ethics Wars Have Undermined American Government, Business, and Society* (New York: Free Press, 1997).

nessed the Ethics in Government Act[6] and the attendant creation of bureaucracies such as the Office of Government Ethics. The Independent Counsel investigations office has become routine, pursuing every administration since its creation. Targets of its inquiries, figures such as President Carter's assistant Hamilton Jordan, have suffered thorough and legally expensive probes before their exoneration.[7] Does the public believe that our federal institutions have become more ethical as a result? No polling data have ever been brought forth to support such a claim.[8]

But I believe that, in addition to disenchantment with governmentally fostered ethical proceedings, there are much older sources of the apparent ethical schizophrenia in the American public. An appropriate frame for viewing the public's ethical stance may lie far beyond the contemporary debate about Clinton's fate in the impeachment proceedings. I believe that our national difficulty in finding a firm terrain of moral consensus reflects some contrary tensions in religious tradition that long predate the American presidency. I refer to these embedded issues as the perennial problems of casuistry, particularly where public figures are involved. But before sketching that story, I will illustrate the depth and power of these conflicting currents through two Christian perspectives on the Clinton issues — those of James M. Wall, Editor of the *Christian Century*, and of Robert L. Jewett, whose essay appears in this volume.

Looking at Wall's stances on the Lewinsky-related Clinton disclosures, one can see that he was severely critical of President Clinton when he first commented on the latter's "defiant and self-protective" apology of August 17, 1998. Without calling for the president's impeachment, he spoke of Clinton's "original deceit and coverup as reprehensible." Like many other commentators, he wrote the more contrite, sincere religious confession and apology for Clinton that he wished he had heard.[9]

---

6. Pub. L., No. 95-521, 92 Stat. 1824 (the statute was passed in 1978; cited in Morgan and Reynolds at 81).

7. Morgan and Reynolds, 77.

8. Cf. Joseph S. Nye, Jr., Philip D. Zelikow, and David C. King, eds., *Why People Don't Trust Government* (Cambridge: Harvard University Press, 1997). See esp. Derek Bok's chapter, "Fall from Grace: The Public's Loss of Faith in Government."

9. James M. Wall, "Unrepentant, Unforgiven," *Christian Century* (August 26–September 2, 1998), 771.

But by the time of the President's Religious Leaders' Prayer Breakfast on September 11, Wall surely spoke as well for many unchurched Americans or even anti-church libertarians when he suggested that "Americans' respect for privacy exceeds their prurient interests." He went on to speculate about the specter of a new theocracy. "Are we witnessing a foretaste of what would happen were the religious and political right to seize total control of government?"[10] Weighing the sins of the contending parties, he invited us to smell the sulphurous odors emanating from the Starr camp: "There has been a violation of human decency that far exceeds the level of sinfulness in the president's sexual encounters."[11] But lest we see Wall's comment as purely secular politics, we should be aware of his account of personally attending the White House Prayer Breakfast at which President Clinton disclosed his program of spiritual regeneration. He reports, "I saw close-up a man and his wife deep in agony over the public shame and humiliation he had brought upon himself, his family, and the nation. . . . It was a remarkable event — a leader caught in the consequences of his confessed sins was reaching out in supplication and asking for forgiveness."[12] Wall was clearly drawn in by the spirit of the pastoral team committed to the President's spiritual rehabilitation. In the context of Wall's trusting and sympathetic judgment, I would like to attach the label "pastoral"[13] to his perspective on the President's situation.

In a different vein, Robert L. Jewett has contemplated the Clinton impeachment issues from much wider historical perspectives. He has laid out some neglected civic ideals of honor for assessing our Presidents, and he sees a radically diminished stature that impairs Clinton's effectiveness as a national leader who requires trusting loyalty from his employees. He also questions whether the ministerial circle of Tony Campolo, Gordon MacDonald, and J. Philip Wogaman are sufficiently clear about the appropriateness of public confession — or whether forgiveness reinstates the right to exercise presidential responsibility. In

10. James M. Wall, "There but for the Grace of God," *Christian Century* (October 14, 1998), 922.

11. Ibid.

12. Ibid.

13. In using the word "pastoral," I designate the role of someone principally concerned with the spiritual care of a parishioner. I do not intend that such a person never has prophetic moments with a congregation or with the larger community.

addition, Jewett has lifted up religious standards that call into question the public piety associated with the President's "accountability circle." Jewett suspects that, in this widely advertised spiritual device, President Clinton has tactically donned a mantle of religiosity to protect himself from the normal consequences for his behavior. In this regard, Jewett is struck by the relevance of a biblical precedent in the story of Jehu, wherein we can discern the dangers of "religious devotion as a form of propaganda."

For my purposes here, I attach the label "prophetic"[14] to Jewett's subtle exposition. Its guiding premise is that American political and ethical judgment has lost touch with certain vital civic ideals and religious insights. Their absence accounts for public apathy and the ease with which Clinton drew the ministers into a protective circle around him.

In the conflict between the "prophetic" response of Jewett and the "pastoral" response of Wall and Clinton's pastoral team, I discern some persistent conflicts over moral casuistry that have driven much of Christianity's own tumultuous history. I believe that current public hesitation to press for sanctions in the Clinton proceedings reflects some of these historical dilemmas about how to apply moral rules to messy cases. If members of the same faith community can be as divided as Wall and Jewett are on this issue, it seems unlikely that a more religiously diverse public can achieve agreement of the sort that terminated Nixon's Presidency during the Watergate episode. In its intractable ambiguities for so many Americans, the Clinton matter may join issues such as abortion, euthanasia, the Vietnam War, affirmative action, and those others that the nation perpetually debated without reaching consensus.

---

14. In using the word "prophetic," I have in mind the Hebrew prophets who so often speak on behalf of God in criticizing the sinfulness of the culture and its failure to remember the laws laid down for them. Just as the word "casuistry" developed negative associations, "prophecy" has a bad flavor when it is a "jeremiad" — meaning an ill-tempered harangue that considers no mitigating circumstances or counterbalancing factors. The Book of Jeremiah contains many condemnations of official power, social injustice, and idolatrous worship. He was arrested and tried on charges relating to his "Temple sermon" in Jeremiah 7:1-15 and also in 26:1-24.

Casuistry

Casuistry is a word with connotations that range from the neutral to the unfavorable; it is rare to hear it tinged with a positive flavor. The von Harnack citation at the beginning of this essay comes from his fervent commentary on Jesuit moral casuistry in the Middle Ages. Figures such as von Harnack, and Pascal more than 200 years before him, made of "casuistry" a term of contempt. In the neutral sense used here, casuistry simply describes the application of general rules or ideals to particular cases.[15] Any system based on abstract commands such as "Honor thy father and thy mother" requires interpretation in particular cases. For example, what is the child's responsibility when parents are exploitative or cruel? And how would we reconcile some commands with others? Suppose your parents insisted that you "bear false witness" for their protection? Applying rules in such complex situations requires attention to competing values and to nuances in the factual circumstances. And resolving the dilemma typically means breaking at least one of the conflicting rules. In cases where the conduct implications of values conflict, as so often happens with love and justice, one value must receive a higher weighting than the other. It's obvious that moral prophecy also applies rules to cases, but the tradition as defined by its chief exemplars in the Hebrew Bible does not reflect a commitment to an ethical balancing act in which mitigating circumstances or countervailing values are foregrounded. The term "jeremiad" developed in the language to characterize an extreme form of moral confrontation, one that is relentlessly negative, prosecutorial in style as it highlights the issues.

Historically, law-based religious traditions exhibit a tension between morally rigorous, prophetic advocates of ideals and the more lax, more flexible posture typical of those who live the ideals or assist others in adapting them. The conflict between law and love, legalism or formalistic casuistry and the loving spirit, is in fact one of the leading themes of Jesus' ministry. The vitality of a religion's ideals surely depends on its moral prophets, but the livability of a religion and the loyalty of ordinary people may largely depend on flexible adaptations of

---

15. Historically, casuistry also meant the discipline of bringing together many "cases of conscience" and studying them to determine factual circumstances and intentions that bear on moral decisions.

abstract principles. Werner Stark, a sociologist of religion, created convenient labels to characterize these conflicting ethical impulses: "rigorism" and "laxism." It corresponds to my contrast between "prophetic" and "pastoral" roles.

According to Stark, "the area in which casuistry first made its appearance was, not surprisingly, the activity of the Church which comes closest to the function and practice of the law — the exercise of discipline, more concretely, the punishment of sins and sinners."[16] A crucial moment arrived with the development of the private confessional. "The emphasis was less on the past, on deeds done, than on the future, the conduct to be expected."[17] As the private confessional developed its own traditions, it appeared that there was "an illicit bending of general principles, if not a playing fast and loose with sacred imperatives."[18] And here were planted the seeds of conflict. Could the private confessional be an arena of rehabilitating love while functioning as a tribunal of ethical law? The difficulty is obvious. As a representative of the morally prophetic tradition, the priest could easily alienate the sinner entirely with a condemning attitude. So, realizing the need to keep the sheep with the flock, the priest as spiritual caregiver could easily "set aside obligations and commandments which must needs be binding on all men."[19]

Blaise Pascal, who pressed the case of the Jansenists against the casuistic tradition of the Jesuits, sarcastically described the church's dilemma in the following way. His monk exclaims, "Alas . . . our main object, no doubt, should have been to establish no other maxims than those of the Gospel in all their strictness." But "men have arrived at such a pitch of corruption nowadays, that unable to make them come to us, we must even go to them, otherwise they would cast us off altogether. . . . The grand project of our Society, for the good of religion, is never to repulse anyone, let him be what he may, and so avoid driving people to despair." Pascal's Jesuit monk goes on to admit that the church has "gentle maxims" that will suit all circumstances and persons, whether they be rich or poor, devout or faithless, married or un-

16. Werner Stark, "Casuistry," I, 258 in Philip P. Wiener, ed., *Dictionary of the History of Ideas: Studies of Selected Pivotal Ideas* (New York: Scribner's, 1973).
17. Stark, 258.
18. Stark, 259.
19. Stark, 259.

married.[20] It is Pascal's skewering portraits of this kind that gave casuistry the bad odor that it has never shaken off.[21]

Though involved with the polemics of a turbulent moment in the history of Catholicism, Pascal clearly points toward the basis for conflicts within *any* religious community. While prophetic figures might urge their comrades to achieve the moral maximum, the practitioners of pastoral casuistry gravitate toward the minimum, trying, in Stark's words, "to draw the lowest acceptable line between ethical and nonethical."[22] Pascal's own Jansenist group eventually made its own wrenching compromises. Many followers were required to openly recant their views on grace and salvation.[23]

This sort of conflict over standards had, of course, been a powerful force during the Protestant Reformation. As Stark points out, when Luther toasted the papal excommunication bull directed at him, he also tossed a casuistic text, *Summa Angelica,* onto the fire.[24] Its association with penances and indulgences earned it a place on Luther's bonfire for corrupt moral practices. Unfortunately for the firmly principled, prophetic Luther, he faced an especially embarrassing casuistic dilemma himself before his career was over. His troublesome pastoral moment came in dealing with a German nobleman, the landgrave Philip of Hesse, who favored the Protestant cause.[25] At the time, the right to be a

---

20. Richard Popkin, ed., *The Provincial Letters (1656-1657),* in *Pascal: Selections* (New York: Scribner-Macmillan, 1989), "Letter VI," 121.

21. Cf. Johann P. Somerville, "The 'New Art of Lying,'" in Edmund Leites, *Conscience and Casuistry in Early Modern Europe* (Cambridge, England: Cambridge University Press, 1988), 159-84. Somerville has made a careful study of both Protestant and Catholic casuistry in responding to St. Augustine's absolute rule against lying. He concludes that despite their attempt to differentiate themselves from one another, their results were comparable. For both, the functional equivalent of lying was acceptable in certain situations.

22. Stark, 260.

23. Cf. Jeannine E. Olson, "Jansenism," *The Oxford Encyclopedia of the Reformation* (New York: Oxford University Press, 1996), II, 332.

24. Stark, 262.

25. The story of Luther and Melanchthon's dealings with Philip is given detailed exposition in Martin Brecht's section "The Calamitous Bigamy of Landgrave Philip," in *Martin Luther: The Preservation of the Church, 1532-1546* (Minneapolis: Fortress Press, 1985), 205-15. It is also related in Heiko A. Oberman, *Luther: Between Man and the Devil* (New Haven: Yale University Press, 1989), 283-89.

Catholic or a Protestant obviously depended on the forbearance of a friendly regional political prince. To Luther as leader, it was obviously a matter of survival that there be such protectors of the emerging faith.

Philip was unhappy with his wife, Christina, who had borne seven children. But he didn't wish to give her up entirely. He just wanted to add a more enticing second wife, Margarethe von der Sala. According to the formally expressed norms of the time, the Catholic nobility, working with their churches, were prepared to punish bigamy with death. Luther's reforms had already pioneered the promotion of a married clergy, but there was never any hint that bigamy was part of his revolution. Philip therefore needed protection from Protestant public opinion by way of approval from Luther, who initially thought the request outrageous. But the resourceful Philip had done his biblical homework, pointing out that the Hebrew patriarchs had several wives. And the New Testament said nothing to forbid bigamy. So why not?

Luther wasn't impressed with Philip's pre-Christian biblical precedents. But as a pastor concerned about Philip's soul and his wayward lust, Luther had to consider whether a second wife was worse than prolonged adulteries from which additional children would likely come. He also had to imagine the possibility that Philip would leave his Christian practice entirely if he didn't get some kind of license to do as he wanted. And while he also thought that bigamy was a terrible example, Luther would have to fear for the future of his movement if he lost Philip's territory.

So Luther finally said yes in a 1539 "confessional counsel" with Philip. As Martin Brecht summarizes the reasoning: "The only possible solution was a secret marriage. . . . The second wife should be kept like a concubine, the way other princes did. This solution was compatible with the gospel, which was concerned about salvation, obedience, and improving depraved nature."[26] Correctly fearing the poor example of such an arrangement for others (as well as their reputations) if the consent were revealed, Luther and Melancthon sought to impose the condition that the marriage "would only be known to a few under the seal of the confessional."[27] They hoped that Philip would just never talk about it. Luther was profoundly unhappy, but rationalized it thus: "It

26. Brecht, 206.
27. Brecht, 206.

was a heavy matter on our hearts, but since we were unable to prevent it, we sought to save his conscience the best we could."[28]

Unfortunately for Luther, the secret escaped through the conversation of Philip's sister and others. Philip's self-protective instinct eventually led him to implore Luther to confirm his pastoral approval. Luther refused, but it seemed to become generally known anyway. Luther was further embarrassed to learn that the landgrave had been having other sexual affairs and remarked that if he had better known Philip's inclinations, "not even an angel would have gotten me to give such advice."[29] The unwelcome disclosure confirmed Catholic opinion that Luther was a scoundrel. Combined with the fact that he, an ex-monk, had married an ex-nun, it was additional evidence that his movement was about surrendering to lust. Protestants themselves felt that it was a dark stain on their integrity. Luther himself soldiered on, undoubtedly somewhat consoled by the fact that Philip did not take Hesse back to Catholic control.

It would be arrogant to tell this story in the belief that our hindsight can trump Luther's uncomfortable decision. It is plausible to conclude that Luther offered the "least worst" pastoral response in a messy situation. But his sympathetic, calculating advice certainly lacked the old clarity of his role as a moral prophet to the Roman church. And his adventure in pastoral casuistry should give pause to anyone who ministers to a powerful political figure. Luther's pastoral casuistry can also serve to help us grasp the perplexities of American public opinion in responding to the President's behavior. There is little dispute about the norms of fidelity, truth telling, and trust that are relevant in judging such cases. Nor is there factual disagreement that those norms have been violated. In these regards, there is a wide consensus about the relevance of prophetically based ideals of conduct.

But questions about accountability and sanctions for Clinton's offenses take us into a more complex territory. Despite its lethargy over the proceedings, American opinion seems willing to weigh the abundant aggravating and mitigating ethical aspects of the situation. Among repeatedly mentioned interpretations that have been weighed in public casuistry are the following:

28. Brecht, 208.
29. Brecht, 208.

1. the President has substantially lost the trust and respect that a President needs to govern, and mere forgiveness can never restore that loss;
2. the President violated his oath of office by conspicuously failing to uphold his constitutional responsibility as the nation's chief law enforcement officer;
3. the President's recklessness in pursuing the affair when he was already under pressure in the Paula Jones affair expresses a character flaw so large that it invites suspicion about his behavior in a national crisis;
4. the President has already been "punished" by prolonged public humiliation that includes his own (apparently contrite) admission of guilt;
5. the President's exposure as an offender depended on entrapment methods (via the secret recordings of Linda Tripp) that may themselves be illegal;
6. the public's perception of an overly intrusive investigation by Kenneth Starr, which many see as motivated by political enmity;
7. the second-tier status of the President's offenses are only indirectly crimes against the nation's laws, since they arose from the desire to conceal a sexual affair rather than from an illegal policy of the state;
8. the fear of political and economic disruption, or the loss of international prestige, should the President be forced from office.

The decision in this case is very unlike the decision a judge makes in imposing a fine for speeding or public littering. There the statutes and precedents allow the judge to decide most cases by referring to what is customarily done in applying the law to the case. The weighing of all these factors is far more like the decisions about divorce that were made by courts before the no-fault era. The innocence and the offenses could be listed for each of the contending parties. But lacking features such as severe cruelty or abandonment, the facts seldom presented themselves in a morally compelling way. The court's decision was, in effect, an act of judgmental faith about the fate of the marriage.

Americans currently seem to have a very complex, if not contradictory, view of the ethical issues in the Clinton matter. They seem to have leaned in the pastoral-casuistic direction, sympathizing with the sinner and suspicious of his most obdurate opponents. They seem to hope that Clinton's announced plan of spiritual repentance and re-newal will allow him to serve the remainder of his term without any new character disasters. David Broder has wisely suggested an enormous psychic cost in adapting to the ethical realities of a Clinton presidency. He reports the efforts of pollster Peter Hart to explore a twelve-member focus group's attempt "to reconcile their condemnation of Clinton's behavior with their disinclination to see him punished." According to Hart, some were so "frustrated that they came close to tears." He concluded: "Every one of them was inconsistent. It tells you how much the country has to work through."[30]

With this sort of anger and tearful anxiety, any "moving on" that simply bypasses issues of presidential responsibility will not serve us well. We can respect the sympathetic impulses and the casuistic balancing that strives so hard to be fair. But the nation will better serve itself with a series of principled judgments that articulate a clear standard for future conduct in the office. Perhaps from this entire painful episode we can form a working ethical consensus that moves beyond accusations, avoidances, and angry tears. That is always the hope of democracy.

30. David Broder. "Hearings Can Help Resolve National Ambivalence." *Austin American Statesman* (November 18, 1998), Section A, p. 15.

Confession and Forgiveness in the Public Sphere: A Biblical Evaluation

ROBERT JEWETT

President Clinton's confessional speeches on August 17 and September 11 raise significant issues for theologians and religious leaders. How are confessions to be evaluated when they occur in a public setting? Do they have an appropriate place in the political arena? The most prominent voices heard thus far provide ready answers to these questions. We have been assured by Rev. Jesse Jackson that officials should be judged on their public performance, not on the revelation of their private behavior — which the country should now be willing to forgive.[1] Donald W. Shriver, the author of *An Ethic for Enemies: Forgiveness in Politics,* argues that the President should be forgiven in order to overcome the effect of evil.[2] In articles published in *The Christian Century,* editor James M. Wall urges his readers to forgive the President, with no further "punishment" applied.[3] Rev. J. Philip

---

1. See Scott Forner, "Rev. Jackson Counsels Mrs. Clinton, Chelsea," *The Chicago Sun-Times* (August 18, 1998), 3; Jackson's talk show of August 23 on CNN developed this same case for forgiveness on biblical grounds.

2. See Steve Kloehn, "To Err Is Clinton, but Is Public Divine?" *The Chicago Tribune* (August 23, 1998), Section 4, p. 2; Donald W. Shriver's book *An Ethic for Enemies: Forgiveness in Politics* was published by Oxford University Press in 1995.

3. James M. Wall, "There but for the Grace of God," *The Christian Century*

Wogaman, pastor of the Foundry United Methodist Church where the Clintons attend, and a distinguished authority on Christian ethics,[4] contends that talk of political penalties is unbiblical: "King David did something that was much worse than anything that President Clinton is alleged to have done. And King David, if I read my Bible correctly, was not impeached."[5]

This matter of reading the Bible "correctly" is precisely what concerns a biblical scholar like me. The biblical view of confession and forgiveness raises serious doubts about these prominent opinions. Moreover, some of the most appropriate biblical materials have not even surfaced in the public discussion. This leads me to begin with the concept of honor in relation to forgiveness, and then to address the question of how biblical categories can provide the basis for evaluating public confessions.

Forgiveness versus Honor

The concept of *honor* has seemed quite distant from discussions within the religious community,[6] but the term belongs to an important complex of biblical ideas concerning public respect and recognition.[7]

(October 14, 1998), 947, 922; see also his editorials "Appalling Behavior," *The Christian Century* (October 7, 1998), 891 and "Punishment for Sin," *The Christian Century* (October 28, 1998), 986: "The entire impeachment process has little chance of doing anything other than make religious moralists happy to see a sinner pay for his sins."

4. See J. Philip Wogaman, *Speaking the Truth in Love: Prophetic Preaching to a Broken World* (Louisville: Westminster John Knox, 1998); *Christian Ethics: A Historical Introduction* (Louisville: Westminster John Knox, 1993).

5. Cited by Richard Roeper, "One Thing's Certain: Clinton Is Sorry, All Right," *The Chicago Sun-Times* (August 18, 1998), 4.

6. While absent from theological discussion of the President's behavior, the concept of honor surfaces in certain arenas of secular discussion; for example, John Brandl, Dean of the University of Minnesota's Humphrey Institute of Public Affairs, used this language in an Op-Ed piece for the *Minneapolis Star-Tribune:* "Clinton can honor public service by resigning" (October 1, 1998). Honor appears to remain decisive in evaluations of the situation within the American military, according to Steve Chapman's report of the controversy caused by Maj. Shane Sellers' letter in a recent *Navy Times:* "When Soldiers Give Clinton a Different Salute," *The Chicago Tribune* (October 25, 1998), Section 1, p. 23.

7. See my study, "Honor and Shame in the Argument of Romans," 257-72

Honor is achieved through the maintenance of integrity (Prov. 8:1-21), speaking the truth without dissimulation: "Let what you say be simply 'Yes' or 'No'; anything more than this comes from evil" (Matt. 5:37). Honorable persons defend the dignity of the weak (2 Cor. 11:28-29), overlooking personal advantage for the sake of the larger community (Judges 5). The honorable are recognized as righteous as well as wise (Prov. 5-6); they respect the community's sense of decency (Phil. 4:8-9). When the community sets its trust in a leader who conforms to these standards, that person is said to be "honorable." There is a particular emphasis throughout the Bible on honoring parents, marital partners, and political leaders, with frequent advice about how such figures should behave so as to warrant being honored. The admonition in Romans 13:7 concerning respect for the government is particularly clear on the matter of warrant: believers are to give "honor to whom honor is due."

In the light of this legacy, how should Christians in a modern democracy act when honor is no longer deserved? This is an issue of much greater public cogency than questions about whether the President should be forgiven. That adultery and prevarication can be forgiven is indisputable — for leaders as well as for common citizens. Whether repentance is genuine remains finally a matter between sinners and God. But forgivability is not a qualification for office. The real question is whether the public should continue to honor someone whose tenure in office has been marred by months of lying. Jean Bethke Elshtain, who teaches political ethics at the Divinity School of the Uni-

---

in A. Brown, G. F. Snyder, and V. Wiles, eds., *Putting Body and Soul Together: Essays in Honor of Robin Scroggs* (Valley Forge: Trinity Press International, 1997). For general background, see David Arthur deSilva, *Despising Shame: Honor Discourse and Community Maintenance in the Epistle to the Hebrews* (Atlanta: Scholars Press, 1995); *idem,* "'Worthy of His Kingdom': Honor Discourse and Social Engineering in 1 Thessalonians," *Journal for the Study of the New Testament* 64 (1996): 49-79; Arthur J. Dewey, "A Matter of Honor: A Social-historical Analysis of 2 Corinthians 10," *Harvard Theological Review* 78 (1985): 209-17; Bruce J. Malina and Jerome H. Neyrey, "Honor and Shame in Luke-Acts: Pivotal Values of the Mediterranean World," in J. H. Neyrey, ed., *The Social World of Luke-Acts: Models for Biblical Interpretation* (Peabody: Hendrickson, 1991), 25-65; Victor H. Matthews and Don C. Benjamin, eds., *Honor and Shame in the World of the Bible,* Semeia 68 (Atlanta: Scholars Press, 1996); Halvor Moxnes, "Honor and Shame," in R. L. Rohrbaugh, ed., *The Social Sciences and New Testament Interpretation* (Peabody: Hendrickson, 1996), 19-40.

versity of Chicago,[8] told a reporter recently: "I'm not in a position to forgive him [Mr. Clinton]. Forgiveness is not a political term. Politically, I make a judgment that there is a bond that has been broken. How many people does he get to slander? How many times does he get to lie, and how many people does he get to lie for him? I think he's reached the limit."[9]

The distinction between a private ethic of forgiveness and a public ethic of honor was more fully understood in earlier American discourse about political office, with its emphasis on the supreme importance of a good name and of maintaining the trust of the electorate.[10] Richard Brookhiser's recent study *Rediscovering George Washington: Founding Father* sketches our first President's "lifelong concern with courtesy and reputation," citing Parson Weems's dictum that it was "no wonder every body honoured him who honoured every body."[11] The young Washington's oft-cited "I cannot tell a lie" fits this framework of deserving public honor. Earlier this year, Douglas L. Wilson published *Honor's Voice: The Transformation of Abraham Lincoln,* which describes our greatest President's struggles as a young man to establish and maintain his honor. After falling into profound melancholy when he feared the loss of "the gem" of his character, his ability to live up to his obligations, he ultimately felt "honor bound" to matrimony with Mary Todd.[12] The young Lincoln received the sobriquet "Honest Abe," and the mature President Lincoln "became known for his resolution" in following policies that he felt were truthful and wise.[13]

In view of the priority of honor in biblical and earlier American discourse about leadership, what are we to say about our current President? That Mr. Clinton entered into an affair with a twenty-two-year-

8. For background, see Jean Bethke Elshtain's recent books, *Augustine and the Limits of Politics* (Notre Dame: University of Notre Dame Press, 1995, 1998); *Democratic Authority at Century's End* (Eugene: University of Oregon Books, 1997); *New Wine and Old Bottles: International Politics and Ethical Discourse* (Notre Dame: University of Notre Dame Press, 1998).

9. Cited in Steve Kloehn, "To Err Is Clinton," 2.

10. See, for example, *Our Sacred Honor: Words of Advice from the Founders in Stories, Letters, Poems, and Speeches* (Nashville: Broadman & Holman, 1997).

11. Richard Brookhiser, *Rediscovering George Washington: Founding Father* (New York: Free Press, 1997), 136, 131.

12. Douglas L. Wilson, *Honor's Voice: The Transformation of Abraham Lincoln* (New York: Knopf, 1998), 265-92, esp. 290.

13. Wilson, *Honor's Voice,* 322.

old intern entrusted to his care in the White House was inherently dishonorable, both on grounds of adultery and of sexual misconduct with an employee of inferior rank, to adapt the language of a military code that the President should know as Commander-in-Chief. But the matter of honor might never have risen to a crisis point without the cloak of lies with which he subsequently sought to disguise his behavior. These lies were public, not restricted to the "private" sphere that the August 17 speech sought to seal from view. They began with misleading statements in legal depositions and categorical denials to the public. They continued as Mr. Clinton enlisted cabinet members, White House staff, members of Congress, and thousands of political leaders throughout the country to support the lie. Clinton even engaged his wife, apparently misinformed about the affair, to employ her immense prestige on his behalf.

Now that the President has acknowledged that lie, each person engaged in this massive distortion of the truth, whether innocently or not, has been swept into dishonor. They are either dupes or deceivers. In either case their credibility has been impaired, and they will carry to their dying day the public stain of having been party to a sordid fraud whose purpose was nothing more elevating than to prevent Mr. Clinton from losing his political reputation and perhaps his position. In seeking to protect his honor, they damaged their own. By ruthlessly enlisting his allies in this campaign of self-serving falsehood, William Jefferson Clinton forfeited a substantial measure of credibility as a responsible political leader.

The dishonor caused by the President's campaign of lies extends to every branch of our public system. The White House staff, which serves as the administrative center of government, focused its energies for months on the task of discrediting evidence and witnesses. The judicial branch was so burdened with attacks on the fairness of the prosecutor that the impartiality of the entire legal system was undermined. The legislative branch of government was led into unseemly squabbles over the spurious question of the President's integrity, causing citizens to lower their respect for Congress. The most serious damage has been done to the fourth estate of our public life, the news media, which has been blamed for a single-minded pursuit of all the sordid details of the truth, almost to the exclusion of the larger issues that should concern the country. By any measure, the level of cynicism about our public institutions has been deepened by these developments. This is all the more despicable because the center of these abrasive controversies was not a matter of policy but of denials about the President's behavior, the essentials of which he has now admitted. A more futile, irresponsible, and corrosive debate spawned by an American President is impossible to recollect.

Mr. Clinton's address to the nation on August 17 failed conspicuously in its effort to recover honor.[14] Since it came only after the prospect of DNA evidence and testimony before the Independent Counsel made it clear that the lie could no longer be maintained, its sincerity as a public admission was fundamentally impaired. The statement overlooked the element of the exploitation of a young employee/intern, a matter that cannot be covered by the claim of "privacy," especially when federal employees are required to avoid such actions. In claiming that his testimony had been "legally accurate," Mr. Clinton's speech maintains spurious legal distinctions that are far from the admonition simply to say "Yes" or "No."[15] That he "at no time" asked "anyone to lie" was intended to deny subornation of perjury in the Monica Lewinsky case; but the statement remains in conflict with months of dishonest propaganda.[16] That the investigation of these lies "has gone on too long, cost too much and hurt too many innocent people" implies that the source of delay has been the Independent Counsel; but Clinton's evasions of the truth, in fact, lie at the heart of this tedious story.

About half of the August 17 address was devoted to a bitter attack on the actions of the Independent Counsel.[17] It was sobering to realize

14. The following citations of the speech come from "Text of Clinton's address," *The Chicago Sun-Times* (August 18, 1998), 6.

15. David Marannis, *The Clinton Enigma: A Four-and-a-Half-Minute Speech Reveals This President's Entire Life* (New York: Simon & Schuster, 1998), 37-40, details the many instances in Clinton's earlier career when "legal accuracy" disguised actual behavior.

16. That these words reappeared in Ms. Lewinsky's comments to the grand jury suggests that they had been rehearsed with Mr. Clinton as a cover story. That this comment was not included in the Starr report to Congress has been decried as an intentional deletion of exculpatory material, according to David E. Rosenbaum, "A View That Starr's Report Is Not Backed by the Facts: The Evidence," *The New York Times* (September 22, 1998), A19. Is the American public naive enough to believe that so skilled a lawyer as Mr. Clinton would have explicitly asked her to lie for him or promised her job in return for such lies?

17. Biographer Marannis explains in *Clinton Enigma* (p. 89) how predict-

that Mr. Clinton's anger over the exposure of his dishonorable actions far outweighed any remorse about the damage he had done. By inviting the public to share his rage, he sought a solidarity in victimage whereby his audience would perceive the alleged evils of critics and prosecutors to outweigh the minor mistakes of folks like himself. This claim to be more honorable than the prosecutor was a cynical evasion of responsibility, particularly for someone who has sworn to uphold the law. The appeal to "turn away from the spectacle of the past seven months" is similarly problematic, despite its wide acceptance by a weary public. What he requests is for the public to join his exemption from accountability and to overlook the lies that have poisoned political discourse. He invites us to a level of cynicism that abandons the links between honor and common decency, between the law and the principle of equal enforcement for all.

As a person who twice voted for Mr. Clinton, I believe that his address on August 17 confirmed that there was no way to restore public trust in his leadership. Some of us may be able to overlook his "personal failure," but we will never believe him again, never respect and honor him as a person of integrity whose word is his bond. In Richard Roeper's words, this speech confirms that "he is a liar. A cheat. A conniver. A manipulator. And we love him."[18] Our ambivalence has prevented some from facing a bitter consequence: since Mr. Clinton will not resign, our only recourse is that he be impeached, because the integrity of our governmental system is now in jeopardy. Without "honor to whom honor is due," there is no possibility of maintaining a democratic system of government, which requires a relationship of "trust and trustworthiness" between leaders and the public.[19] More-

---

able this attack was in the light of Mr. Clinton's earlier career: it was the "result of a personality that explained and rationalized compulsively; that tended ever to the political strategy of attacking his attackers, believing that everything is political and that politics is war. . . ."

18. Roeper, "Clinton Is Sorry, All Right," 4.

19. Political scientist Stanley A. Renshon develops this theme in *High Hopes: The Clinton Presidency and the Politics of Ambition,* 2d ed. (New York/London: Routledge, 1998), 256-57: "If presidential leadership is essentially a relationship, then at its heart lie trust and trustworthiness. Trust and trustworthiness are the psychological foundation of the citizen-leader relationship. In giving their trust, citizens bestow legitimacy. In being trustworthy, leaders earn it." He argues that when this trust is violated, "the fabric of democracy is in danger as the psychological adhesive that holds it together loosens."

over, a liar as the nation's chief role model does incalculable damage to the honorable commitments that are the invisible glue that sustains a free and prosperous society.

Perhaps our ambivalence would be modified by imagining what would happen if our bankers and stockbrokers and business executives followed Clinton's example of self-serving dishonesty; if our teachers and scientists and doctors and law enforcement officials were led to abandon their ideal of commitment to the honest truth; if our journalists and clergy dropped their standards of truthful integrity. Nothing is more central to the biblical message than the belief that falsity is self-destructive and cannot endure. "Truthful lips endure for ever, but a lying tongue is but for a moment" (Prov. 12:19). Our system can readily survive the departure of a brilliant political leader who has forfeited public trust. But we cannot survive the abandonment of trust itself.

Confession as Propaganda

The explicitly religious confession at the Religious Leaders' Prayer Breakfast in the White House on September 11, 1998, and the subsequent publicizing of pastoral counseling sessions for the President, pose a separate challenge to the integrity of religion, particularly when one takes biblical insights into account. In response to the concerns raised by Senator Joseph Lieberman and various voices within the religious community, the President skillfully cited Jewish and Christian statements concerning repentance, presenting himself as genuinely sorry. But in describing what such repentance implies for his behavior, he began with the item that seems to stand at the top of his priorities: "First, I will instruct my lawyers to mount a vigorous defense, using all available appropriate arguments, but legal language must not obscure the fact that I have done wrong."[20] This defense entails *denying* the very acts that the confession seemingly *admits*. Since this statement about what is "first" correlates with frequent references to the prayer breakfast by his defenders and the President himself, and since Mr. Clinton's sincerity is authenticated by publicly announced sessions with pastoral

20. "President Clinton's Address at the National Prayer Breakfast," *The New York Times* (September 12, 1998), A10.

60

counselors, it raises a question whether this is a repentance in the service of a defense strategy.[21]

The dangers of a public demonstration of religious devotion have been explored by the Hebrew prophets and Jesus of Nazareth. The latter urged praying in the privacy of one's "closet" rather than on the "street corner," to counter the motivation to "be seen by men" (Matt. 6:56). The President's actions are reminiscent of Jehu's invitation to a popular prophet at the time of the purge of the Omride dynasty. As Jehu drives his chariot through the Plain of Jezreel toward Samaria to kill the remaining members of the royal family, he invites the prophet Jehonadab to ride along: "Come with me, and see my zeal for the Lord" (2 Kings 10:16). An influential religious leader was thus co-opted into giving the public impression that the political purge was religiously motivated and divinely authorized. In fact, it was nothing more than a military coup, which had terrible, long-term consequences for Israel. The prophet Hosea looked back on these events that corrupted both religion and politics and issued the oracle of punishment of national disaster on "the house of Jehu for the blood of Jezreel" (Hosea 1:4). In the present circumstances, President Clinton's public devotion poses no immediate threat of violence as did that of Jehu, but it seems similar in using religious devotion as a form of propaganda.

How can this matter be addressed? One thing is clear: in assessing the authenticity of Mr. Clinton's confession, we should not attempt to enter the sphere of his relationship with God or the state of his soul. Those areas are beyond our knowing. But since the confession was designed for the "street corner," presented from an open "chariot" visible to the entire world through televised images, we are entitled to evaluate it as a public performance. There is no doubt that it was compelling to watch. As one of the participants in the Prayer Breakfast told Andy Shaw of the ABC News Station in Chicago, in answer to the question about whether this was simply a cynical use of religion, "If so, he should be impeached and receive an Oscar at the same time."[22] Since

---

21. Various names have been attached to this event: "Presidential Prayer Breakfast," "National Prayer Breakfast," or "Prayer Breakfast," but according to Maureen Shea in the Office of Public Liaison in the White House, who coordinated the event, the correct name is "Religious Leaders' Breakfast." The clergy participants were invited by the White House to attend this session.

22. John T. Pawlikowski, e-mail message on 22 September 1998, cited by permission: "Yes, I was a participant in the Prayer Breakfast at the White House.

Mr. Clinton may be the most accomplished liar ever to hold the American presidency,[23] capable of making categorical denials to the public and in court procedures concerning allegations he now acknowledges to be true, and maintaining that fiction for months on end, there is no way to be certain that he is now sincere. Therefore, I am forced to rely on more publicly accessible criteria informed by the tradition of biblical ethics.

1. Where did the confession occur and for what audience was it intended? As I noted above, there is a particular concern in the Bible for the proper location of acts of religious devotion. In the technical sense, "confession of sins" belongs within communities of faith[24] or in the private relationship between believers and God.[25] The appropriate audiences for such confessions are therefore God and/or the community of faith. In the case of the early church, such matters were to be taken up within a small circle of believers; only when reconciliation could not be achieved was the entire church to become involved.[26] No-

---

The President seemed genuinely contrite. I was asked afterwards by Andy Shaw of Channel 7 whether this was simply a cynical use of religion. My response was that, if so, he should be impeached and receive an Oscar at the same time. He certainly appeared to be persuasive even though I recognize he knows how to handle media. After the press left we all had the opportunity to speak to him personally as well as to Hillary. Again he seemed genuine. There were a number of people, especially African-American church leaders, who spoke about the need to interject a notion of restorative justice into the public discussion of this situation. Some also said this could be a healing moment for the nation. It is obvious the press is totally incapable of dealing with pastoral notions such as 'restorative justice,' which is being discussed more and more in connection with our penal system. I remain convinced from my experience that religious groups have a real challenge facing them in trying to introduce pastoral notions into public policy decisions."

23. Senator Bob Kerry's comment is apt, particularly because it comes from a prominent Democrat: "Clinton's an unusually good liar. Unusually good." Cited by William J. Bennett, *The Death of Outrage: Bill Clinton and the Assault on American Ideals* (New York: Free Press, 1998), 46. See also Marannis, *Clinton Enigma*, 70-75; Renshon, *High Hopes*, 71-72, 271-72, 275-76, 297-98, 304.

24. See the use of *homologeomai* in 1 John 1:9; Raymond E. Brown, *The Epistles of John: A New Translation with Introduction and Commentary*, Anchor Bible 30 (Garden City: Doubleday, 1982), 208, discusses the "liturgical context" within the church where such confessions were to occur.

25. See Neh. 1:6; Ps. 32:1-5; Dan. 9:3-23.

26. See Matt. 18:15-20, discussed by Eduard Schweizer, *The Good News According to Matthew*, trans. D. E. Green (Atlanta: Knox, 1975), 370-71.

where is there a suggestion that such confessions were to occur in the public sphere beyond the church. This preference for restricting the circle of hearers in order to preserve a measure of privacy and to reduce the temptation of public performances is reflected in the Roman Catholic practice of priests hearing confessions in a private and confidential setting.[27] In ordinary Christian usage, therefore, a "confession of sins" such as occurred before the cameras at the White House Prayer Breakfast on September 11 should properly have occurred in Mr. Clinton's own church or within the privacy of his "closet."

The term "apology" is ordinarily used for expressions of regret or self-defense within the non-religious contexts of government, business, or personal relationships. In the New Testament the word "apology" usually carries the connotation of a defense speech before a court or other accusers.[28] In usage not paralleled in the Bible, the word "apology" began to be used in the late sixteenth century in reference to "an explanation offered to a person affected by one's action that no offense was intended, coupled with an expression of regret for any that may have been given; or, a frank acknowledgement of the offense with expression of regret for it, by way of reparation."[29] While a confession of sins assumes the primary offense was against God, an apology assumes a strictly human offense, whether against an individual, an institution, or against the law itself. The appropriate responses to an apology are significantly different from responses to a confession of sins: the latter ordinarily evokes from believers a response of unquestioning forgiveness, while an apology can either be accepted or rejected. These distinctions are muddled in Walter Wink's recent discussion, which asserts that Christians are obligated to forgive Mr. Clinton's "apology" while noting instances in which other public "apologies" have been either received or refused, with perfect justification.[30]

27. See Stephan Richter, *Metanoia: Christian Penance and Confession,* trans. R. T. Kelly (New York: Sheed and Ward, 1966), 64-67.
28. See Acts 22:1; 24:10; 25:8, 16; 26:1, 2, 24; 2 Tim. 4:16; 1 Cor. 9:3; 2 Cor. 12:19 as discussed by Ulrich Kellermann in *"apologeomai, apologia,"* *Exegetical Dictionary of the New Testament,* I (1990), 137.
29. *Oxford English Dictionary,* I.389.
30. Walter Wink, "Excuse Me! Apology in Statecraft," *The Christian Century* (October 21, 1998), 956-57, drawn from a forthcoming book with Fortress Press, *When the Powers Fall: Reconciliation in the Healing of the Nations.* Wink refers to Mr. Clinton's "apology" to the American people and argues that "if we are

The distinction between "confession" and "apology" is useful in evaluating what occurred at the Prayer Breakfast. By placing his remarks in the language of confession of sins, Mr. Clinton placed an obligation on believers to accept him at his word and to offer immediate forgiveness. The majority of those present at the Prayer Breakfast reportedly responded in precisely that way,[31] and many believers who witnessed the event on television instinctively followed suit. To raise questions about such a confession seemed to reflect doubt about the mercy of God or imply joining "that army of cynics . . . who cannot accept a plea for forgiveness at face value," in the words of Tony Campolo, one of the ministers who agreed to counsel the President after the Prayer Breakfast.[32] If Mr. Clinton had formulated his remarks in the form of a public apology, no such automatic responses would have been expected. It would have been legitimate to assess whether the apology was sincere, whether it should be accepted, or whether it should be rejected. No categorical aspersions could have been cast on those who made such evaluations, because an apology lacks the sanctified aura of a "confession of sins." When Mr. Clinton made such a confession in a private letter to Immanuel Baptist Church in Little Rock in late October, a church of which he is a member, his message was properly received and absolution was extended, without anyone outside of the congregation reading the details.[33] This, finally, was the proper

---

to imitate God, then we must forgive him." But Wink notes with approval that the apology of the bombardier who dropped the bomb on Nagasaki "was refused by city officers," that the "formal apology" of a Canadian church was "acknowledged" but not accepted by Native American authorities.

31. See Joretta Purdue, "Forgiving a President: Religious Leaders Tell of Giving Clinton Absolution after Prayer Breakfast Confession," *Northern Illinois Conference United Methodist Reporter* (September 25, 1998), who cites Dr. J. Philip Wogaman's observation that the response of the more than 100 guests at the event was "almost uniformly positive and supportive." United Methodist Bishop James K. Matthews said, "There seemed to be a mood there that morning to offer him absolution; and, indeed, when I spoke to him personally, I did speak words of absolution to him." Dr. James Forbes, pastor of Riverside Church in New York City, described his benediction after the President's speech as "a holy moment. . . . I have never seen anything like this in public life."

32. Drawn from a CNN/AllPolitics report on the Internet, September 15, 1998, from a statement released by Eastern College, where Prof. Campolo teaches.

33. "President's Letter to His Home Baptist Church Asks Forgiveness," *The Chicago Tribune* (October 23, 1998), Section 1, 25.

arena for Mr. Clinton's religious confession. But a confession of sins was inappropriate both in form and audience at a nationally televised White House event. The Prayer Breakfast speech treated the nation as if it were a church. By attempting to coerce public acceptance of a false situation, it turned confession into propaganda.

2. What was repented? And do the President's subsequent actions reflect contrition that would confirm his sincerity? An evaluation on this latter issue has already been provided by key religious leaders. In response to Mr. Clinton's version of Jehu's invitation, "Come with me, and see my repentance before the Lord," several pastors have already agreed to play the role of Jehonadab.[34] Their counseling would be a matter to celebrate but for the White House announcement of their pastoral role with the President: the only motivation I can discern in the White House's making these pastoral arrangements public was to aid in the defense strategy. In statements made to television news programs before the counseling sessions were well underway, they provided support on the crucial question of the authenticity of Mr. Clinton's confession. According to Kenneth L. Woodward, these statements conveyed to the American public that "all three think Clinton's studied confession was 'sincere' and 'from the heart.'"[35] One of them went much farther than vouching for Clinton's repentance: J. Philip Wogaman's public statements make it clear that he "does not think the President should resign or be impeached. To demand either would be judgmental because we are all sinners."[36]

Whatever the motivations or views of these counselors, their silence about the precise details of their pastoral sessions, or the rigor of their pastoral interventions, these weekly meetings with the President will provide ongoing proof to the public that Mr. Clinton is truly repentant, despite any of his actions to the contrary. By inviting prominent

34. Laurie Goodstein's article, "Clinton Selects Clerics to Give Him Guidance," *The New York Times* (September 15, 1998), A1, 22, makes it clear that Mr. Clinton selected these ministers and invited them to serve as an "accountability circle," as the White House confirmed.

35. Kenneth L. Woodward, "The Road to Repentance," *Newsweek* (September 28, 1998), 44.

36. Woodward, "Repentance," 44; it should be acknowledged, however, that Wogaman has retained strict confidentiality in his pastoral relationship with Mr. Clinton, refusing to acknowledge that he is meeting privately to discuss these matters.

religious leaders to deal with his confession, Mr. Clinton managed to bring the "closet" of private devotion out onto the street corner "that it may be seen by men." This exploitation of the prestige of sincere religious leaders and of the sanctity of pastoral relationships is a painful reminder of the dangers of Jehu's chariot. There is no record that Jehonadab reported what he saw from the chariot, or made speeches in favor of the coup; his presence alongside Jehu sufficed to imply support.

In place of this categorical authentication, which can so readily serve a propagandistic purpose, we need a more penetrating appraisal. In the biblical tradition, repentance implies an acknowledgment of one's sinful deeds and attitudes,[37] a renunciation of irresponsible behavior, and a return to a healthy relationship with God and one's fellow humans.[38] Nowhere is it suggested that even the most sincere confession relieves persons of consequences or legal liabilities for their evil actions. So what exactly did Mr. Clinton confess to having done? Since he was at pains to point out that he handwrote the speech the night before the Prayer Breakfast, this is the most direct evidence available of the shape of his contrition. In studying this speech a few weeks after it was delivered with such moving pathos, I was struck by its astonishing vagueness. While admitting that "I have sinned," Clinton specifies no action. The only detail he mentions is that people "were hurt," but this is formulated in the passive so that it remains unclear whether he caused it or whether they simply took offense at his innocently intended actions. In rhetoric consistent with the popularly evasive bumper stickers often seen in recent years, "Shit happens," the President confesses the following:

> It is important to me that everybody who has been hurt know that the sorrow I feel is genuine: first, and most important, my family; also my

---

37. In *"metanoia," Exegetical Dictionary of the New Testament,* II (1991), 416, Helmut Merklein observes that the Hebrew prophets stressed "the idea of turning away from (individual) sins," as in Ezek. 14:6 and 18:30. See, for example, Acts 8:22, where Simon Magus is urged to repent from his effort to buy the Holy Spirit: "Repent therefore of this wickedness of yours, and pray to the Lord that, if possible, the intent of your heart may be forgiven you." The prophetess Jezebel is charged with refusing "to repent of her immorality" in Rev. 2:22.

38. See Merklein, *"metanoia,"* 416-19; the idea of repentance as turning to a new beginning in relation to God is developed by J. J. Petuchowski, "The Concept of 'Teshuvah,'" *Judaism* 17 (1968), 175-85.

friends; my staff; my Cabinet; Monica Lewinsky and her family, and the American people.[39]

The President's concern here is not with taking responsibility for any specific acts but in conveying to the public the emotional quality of his "sorrow." Later in the speech, Mr. Clinton details the traits he wishes to cultivate in the future:

> a willingness to give the very forgiveness I seek, a renunciation of the pride and the anger which cloud judgment, lead people to excuse and compare and to blame and complain. Now, what does all this mean, for me and for us?

Mr. Clinton makes no direct admission here that he has been subject to pride or anger or that he has been inclined to blame others; these moral faults are generalized in a sermonic manner as characteristic of "people," of "us." The speech goes on to express gratitude for those "who say that in this case and many others the bounds of privacy have been excessively and unwisely invaded. That may be." This continues the evasion of responsibility that we noted in the August 17 speech, which implicitly blames the Special Prosecutor for violating his mandate by invading the ordinarily protected realm of privacy that any American citizen should enjoy. In contrast to the specificity of this charge, the following sentence reiterates the vague admission: "I still sinned." Mr. Clinton then lifts up the hope that "good can come of this for our country as well as for me and my family." The last third of the speech consists of religious sentiments concerning repentance that evoked powerful reminiscences with the ecclesiastical audience, but admitted of no specific sin. Taken as a whole, this speech is sermonic rather than confessional; it evokes religious sentiments but admits not a single sinful act. Despite the religious language, this is even more evasive than the August 17 speech, because at least there he admitted, "I did have a relationship with Ms. Lewinsky that was not appropriate" and "I misled people, including even my wife."[40]

Mr. Clinton's actions and the responses of his lawyers acting under his direction subsequent to the September 11 "confession" confirm

39. See "President Clinton's Address at the National Prayer Breakfast," *The New York Times* (September 12, 1998), A10.
40. "Text of Clinton's Address," 6.

the impression of an evasion of responsibility. While admitting "an inappropriate sexual relationship with Ms. Lewinsky," the response of the White House lawyers on September 12 was a continuation of denial that Mr. Clinton lied about this in his deposition of January 17, 1998, or in his grand jury testimony on August 17, 1998. "It is, however, the President's good faith and reasonable interpretation that oral sex was outside the special definition of sexual relations provided to him."[41] The denial to the grand jury that "the President touched Ms. Lewinsky's breasts or genitalia" also did not apparently constitute perjury because of this special definition. That Mr. Clinton lied about the "timing of his relationship with Ms. Lewinsky" is deemed "frivolous," although his claim that it began in January 1996 (after she finished her White House internship) was disproven by her testimony and other evidence. The President's denials that he had ever been alone with Ms. Lewinsky are set aside on the grounds that the "lawyers never asked the President whether he was alone with Ms. Lewinsky in the study,"[42] which maintains the fiction that since there were other people in the White House at the time, he could not by definition have ever been alone with her. This evasion is consistent with the denial that Clinton and Lewinsky had conspired to deny their relationship in the legal affidavit she submitted to the judge in the Jones trial because the President "never told Ms. Lewinsky what to say."[43] Likewise, he never "ordered or directed anyone to assist Ms. Lewinsky" in finding a job, although his close friend Vernon Jordan took extraordinary measures in her behalf and reported "mission accomplished" to the President when it was completed. In none of these instances was the President in any way responsible, although the lawyers repeatedly acknowledge that "the President has admitted he had an improper relationship with Ms. Lewinsky. He has apologized. The wrongfulness of that relationship is not in dispute."[44] The confession of sins on September 11 thus stands at the center of his defense strategy: he has sinned, done wrong, but is not liable for any specific act. The defense concludes with this summary: "The President did not commit perjury. He did not obstruct justice. He did not tamper with witnesses. And he did not abuse the power of the

41. "Response of President's Lawyers to Independent Counsel's Report," *The New York Times* (September 14, 1998), A14.
42. *Ibid.*
43. *Ibid.* See also note 16 above.
44. "Response of President's Lawyers," A14.

office of the Presidency."[45] In other words, the entire case against him is a politically motivated effort to "damage" and "embarrass" the President. He is an innocent who may inadvertently have hurt others, is sorry about it, and is justified in moving on as if nothing serious had occurred.

In the news conference with Václav Havel on September 16, Mr. Clinton reiterated the crucial role of the Prayer Breakfast confession in averting any liability or accountability for the "details" of this case:

> On last Friday at the Prayer Breakfast I laid out as carefully and as brutally honestly as I could what I believed the essential truth to be. I also said then and I will say again that I think that the right thing for our country and the right thing for all people concerned is not to get mired in all the details here, but to focus, for me to focus on what I did, to acknowledge it, to atone for it and then to work on my family, where I still have a lot of work to do, difficult work. And to lead this country to deal with the agenda before us. . . .[46]

This statement is the revealing climax of a propagandistic form of confession. The "essential truth" that the public should know is that Bill Clinton has "sinned" just as the rest of the human race has, but that to admit any specific act is to get mired in details that distract the country from its larger responsibilities. What happened at the Prayer Breakfast insulates him from further liability. What remains now is to play the role of the humble servant of the country, which he has played ever since:

> I believe the right thing for the country and what I believe the people of the country want, is now that they know what happened, they want to put it behind them, and they want to go on and they want me to go on and do my job. . . . That is the right thing to do.[47]

---

45. *Ibid.*, final paragraph.

46. "Excerpts from the President's News Conference," *The New York Times* (September 17, 1998), A22.

47. *Ibid.* See also Roger Simon, "Mideast Accord Helps Clinton 'Atone,'" *Chicago Tribune* (October 29, 1998), Section 1, 4: "I'm not trying to sugar-coat the fact that I made a mistake and that I didn't want anybody to know about it," Clinton said, occasionally placing his hand over his heart. "The American people have had quite a decent amount of exposure to that. I hope very much that they have seen that I'm doing my best to atone for it."

This is so high-minded and smooth a statement that it disguises its deviation from the truthful demands of repentance. To repent in the biblical sense is to cease looking at the big picture of how well-intentioned we all are, how much we really want to help others, and how wonderful it would be if everyone accepted our ideals. Repentance is finally to acknowledge, in a moment of transforming truthfulness, the deeds that we have actually committed. Without specificity in acknowledging responsibility for sinful deeds, repentance becomes a hollow manipulation, the kind of religious exercise decried by the biblical prophets and Jesus of Nazareth.[48]

The sad truth that should be confessed is that Mr. Clinton entered into a debased relationship of sexual servicing in the Oval Office, that he lied about it and caused his entire administration to lie about it, that he obstructed justice in sponsoring false statements in legal proceedings and in seeking to suppress evidence. Yet down to the present moment he denies any liability for these acts. He has shown no contrition for undermining our national principle of equality before the law because he has evaded any penalty for the very misconduct for which officers in the armed forces are court-martialed and average citizens "are prosecuted every year by his own Justice Department."[49] He has shown no recognition of the contradiction between his "efforts to lead our country and the world toward peace and freedom, prosperity and harmony"[50] and the unholy war he has unleashed between his defenders and critics since January 1998, which will now continue for months to come. None of his remarks has given the slightest indication of contrition for having debased political discourse through this sordid misuse of presidential powers and rhetoric. In Maureen Dowd's words, his propagandistic evasions have made "Washington Orwellian. His corrupt language corrupts thought." Dowd goes on to observe aptly that "Mr. Clinton's supporters are upset that he did not give his groveling prayer breakfast speech 25 days earlier, on the night he made his defiant television address. But the petulant and angry TV address was the authentic

---

48. For example, see Amos 4:4-5; 5:21-24; Micah 6:1-16; Hosea 10:1-6; Matt. 23:13-36.

49. Jonathan Turley, "Witnesses for the Prosecution," *The Chicago Tribune* (August 30, 1998), Section 1, 19.

50. "National Prayer Breakfast," A10.

Clinton moment. The repentant and lip-biting prayer breakfast speech was the contrived Clinton moment."[51]

To me, however, the most troublesome aspect of this contrivance is that so many people in the religious community have been misled by it. By turning confession into propaganda, President Clinton has disarmed our critical capacities and rendered us vulnerable to the big lie.

Conclusion

Mr. Clinton's public confession and appeal for forgiveness and forgetfulness have the capacity to discredit some of the most delicate and precious aspects of the American religious heritage: compassion, the willingness to forgive, and the inclination to hope for redemption. These are extraordinarily vulnerable traits because they are so innately counterintuitive, so alien to the hostile instincts of the human heart, and so hard to defend when confronted with issues of public justice and accountability. Yet there are no traits more valuable in sustaining a humane society. There is something distinctively American about our capacity for these attitudes — which, of course, does not diminish our other great national faults. But when public willingness to forgive is exploited to avoid genuine accountability, forgiveness itself is discredited. When compassion is evoked to excuse the abuse of power, a holy virtue is made to appear as a vice. When redemption is touted for political advantages, its hope becomes hollow and dishonest. Mr. Clinton's proposal that his repentance should become the model "for the children of this country"[52] is the outrageous climax in this Prayer Breakfast that turned repentance into propaganda. If his continuing assault on moral and religious integrity remains unchallenged, it could have even more grievous effects on our public life than the scars left by an impeachment process.[53]

51. Maureen Dowd, "The Wizard of Is," *The New York Times* (September 16, 1998), A29.

52. "National Prayer Breakfast," A10.

53. The material in this article is adapted from "Confession as Propaganda," *Pro Ecclesia* (Fall, 1998), 395-97, and "The Abandonment of Trust: A Biblical Reflection on Public Lies," *Sojourners* (November-December, 1998), 10-11. Both articles are adapted by permission.

How Shall We Respond to Wrongdoing? Is Moral Indignation Permissible for Christians?

KLYNE SNODGRASS

Unchecked, we are all capable of heinous wrongdoing. Among the basic tasks of society are the prevention and control of and the response to evil and wrong. Our defense systems, police forces, courts, and prisons are only the most obvious efforts to deal with wrong inflicted by self-evident enemies and criminals. But how should we respond to evil and wrongdoing when the perpetrator is one of us — not a malicious criminal, but someone engaged in making the society work? Do we avoid the issue because we all are sinners and say that no one is perfect? Is moral indignation permitted for Christians?

Like most of the nation, I am angered by President Clinton's reckless conduct and disregard both for standards of decency and for the welfare of this country. However, I am less concerned with what happens to Bill Clinton than I am with what happens to *us* as we respond to wrong. Any attempt to disregard Clinton's wrongdoing, to whitewash its effect, or to get this behind us will have long-lasting negative consequences. As Gail Sheehy comments with regard to passages in life, issues pushed down in one period tend to swing up in the next with an added wallop.[1] If we do not deal with this now, we will deal with it later, possibly with more disastrous effects. I am primarily concerned with what we teach ourselves and our children about right and wrong and about how we should respond to wrongdoing. If we pay little attention to immoral acts, we endanger the society's moral awareness. As Cato the Elder pointed out two hundred years before Christ, "Those who rob virtue of honor rob youth of virtue."[2]

I am especially concerned that biblical ideas and passages are co-opted and naively used in irresponsible ways by religious leaders or by the society in general to lessen moral accountability. The Bible has even been used to avoid taking sin seriously. When we use the Bible to avoid substantive response to wrong, we demean everything the Bible stands for. Of course, the Bible has a long history of being abused.

Specifically, I wish to draw attention to President Clinton's defenders' misuse of the analogy of David's sin with Bathsheba in 2 Samuel 11; to the use of the statement "Let him who is without sin cast the first stone," which is taken from a text dealing with an adulterous woman (John 8:3-11); and to *the* primary text on forgiveness, the Parable of the Unforgiving Servant in Matthew 18:23-35.

Before dealing with these texts, however, I wish to give a more general treatment of the issues pertinent to the question of how we should respond to evil. I have no desire to be vindictive or judgmental and am as weary as anyone of hearing of these matters. I wish that none of this obnoxious material had become public. I also wish that a special prosecutor had not been necessary, and, if necessary, did not (fairly or unfairly) stand accused of being biased. I especially wish that Clinton had not violated every standard of decency we know. But once the information has been forced upon us, can we ignore wrongdoing?

Why has there been so little *substantive* response? Does "I am sorry" suffice to rectify the injustices perpetrated on the persons involved and this whole society? We all know that the actions of the President would not be tolerated by any corporate CEO; nor would they be tolerated if they were committed by a corporate CEO. Such a wrongdoer would be liable to a civil suit for damages on the basis of sexual misconduct. Clinton's actions toward women are predatory. Why have

---

1. *Passages* (Toronto: Bantam Books, 1977), 363.
2. See Plutarch's *Moralia* 3.198F, *Sayings of Romans;* Cato the Elder 12; see also Cato the Elder 8: ". . . the worst ruler is one who cannot rule himself."

feminists not responded to this wrongdoing? Why did no one in the Clinton administration who had been told a lie resign? Why do many African-American leaders who support Clinton's policies at the same time appear to ignore his sins? Can we really say, "It is wrong, but so what?"

I lament the fact that this and every discussion is turned into a bipartisan debate. Is the lack of response to evil only because we like the opponents less? When do we as a people stand for something ourselves rather than being manipulated by bipartisan politics? How have we become an unkind people with the idea that "attack" is the best response to cover our faults? Is Washington itself the cancer of the country in that integrity can no longer find lodging there? One can begin to understand how Islamic nations might feel justified in describing the United States as the great Satan, especially with questions swirling over the legitimacy of bombing Sudan and Afghanistan in the midst of the President's problems with the Special Prosecutor and the Lewinsky scandal. If Clinton cannot be believed by his supporters, how can he lead among his enemies?

The culpability, however, has broadened from Clinton to the society as a whole. The issue is no longer that Clinton did something wrong; the issue is whether we care about wrong enough to deal with it, especially when dealing with it is unpleasant, which it always is. Can we tolerate either in a President or in ourselves the legalistic casuistry that requires parsing of the word "is" or that rationalizes behavior that most twelve-year-old kids know is wrong?[3]

It will not do to blame Clinton's conduct and his casuistry on his Southern Baptist upbringing, even if there is some justification for the charge.[4] Southern Baptists often are a caricature of themselves, especially when they distort the gospel to mean "make a decision and you go to heaven, no matter what you do," or place so much focus on individualism that one can interpret Scripture in any way one pleases. As a Southern Baptist who has argued against such distortions for thirty-five years, I assert that even Southern Baptists who communicate such ideas know this is a caricature of Southern Baptist theology. Such

---

3. One cannot help but think of the emphases in the Sermon on the Mount on truth and sexual integrity. See Matt. 5:37 and 27-28.

4. See Ken Woodward, "Sex, Sin, and Salvation," *Newsweek* (Nov. 2, 1998), 37.

"cheap grace" may make us feel good temporarily, but it has little to do with the New Testament. Neither Jesus (who does not speak of grace, but embodies it) nor Paul (who focuses on grace more than anyone) knows anything of cheap grace, as is evident from a glance at Jesus' Sermon on the Mount or Paul's theology of grace as transforming power. Is our attraction to cheap grace the result of the fact that we are not ready for the demands of real grace?

Some enlightening parallels to the Clinton affair bear reflection as we seek avenues to respond to sin. Jimmy Swaggart's escapades brought formal discipline from his denomination and blistering ridicule from the public. After a short time he returned to a greatly reduced ministry, but the legitimacy of his return is still questioned. Newt Gingrich's problems have been virtually overlooked. Mike Tyson's license to box was revoked after he bit off part of Evander Holyfield's ear, but it was reissued after a short time. More recently, Henry J. Lyons, president of the National Baptist Convention USA, was forgiven *unanimously* by the NBC's 195 board members and allowed to remain in office despite admitting to an inappropriate relationship with a female employee, despite his wife's setting fire to a $700,000 home Lyons owned with yet another woman, and despite the fact that he is under indictment for racketeering, grand theft, fraud, extortion, and other crimes. Lyons has announced his intention to run for re-election.[5] Why are we so often tolerant of wrong done by leaders? Is it merely that dealing with the wrong is inconvenient for us? Or what of Augusto Pinochet, the Chilean dictator responsible for so much torture and death? Can we argue, as some do, that leaders should not be held liable for their wrong? God forbid. No one is above the law.

Part of being created in the image of God involves being enlisted in the creative process. For good or ill, we help create the worlds in which we will live. What kind of world shall we create for ourselves? The more we accept lying, sexual misconduct, and other wrongs, the less livable our world becomes. The message in Washington, that everyone lies and that everyone lies about sex, is neither true nor tolerable. We cannot say Clinton's sins were *merely* sexual sins and "innocent" lies. His actions were morally reprehensible and an assault on the truth. To fail to respond substantively to Clinton's moral failure is to lower standards of behavior beyond measure.

5. See *Christianity Today* (October 26, 1998), 16.

The Dangers of Responding to Evil

There are, of course, dangers inherent in responding to evil. Obviously, any accusation or call for justice can lead to an attack from the wrongdoer or others. Specifically, with regard to Clinton's problem, to ask for a substantive recognition of his wrongdoing opens one to the charge of involvement in partisan politics, even if one is not active politically. One may be accused of "sexual witchhunting" and of being vindictive, judgmental, and even un-Christian — certainly charges that no Christian wants to hear. But is it possible to raise a complaint about morals without being viewed as a political partisan or identified with the religious right? Is moral indignation permitted for Christians, or does the Christian focus on forgiveness and grace preclude the kind of prophetic denunciation one finds with Amos or Nathan? Or is the problem that we, especially academics, are so concerned about how we ourselves are viewed and treated that we do not risk speaking at all?

Responding to evil is dangerous for a much larger reason than that it opens one to attack. Responding to evil is dangerous because of what the response may do to *us*. That is why Jesus often says, in effect, "Look to yourself first." No legitimate response to evil is possible without humility and self-awareness; because often, in battling evil, we become evil ourselves. We become the very thing we hate. As Walter Wink points out, quoting Jung and Nietzsche, "You always become the thing you fight the most," and "Whoever fights monsters should see to it that in the process he does not become a monster."[6] We understand this well when we see pro-life advocates become snipers who kill abortion doctors, but it happens in much less obvious ways as well.

Yet, while recognizing the dangers, I would argue that we must respond to evil in substantive ways. Society's reaction to immoral acts must be neither dismissive nor vindictive, neither cavalier nor judgmental. Our reaction must repudiate the wrong and deal with the consequences that inevitably follow immoral acts, all the while seeking reform and restoration for the guilty person. Surely it is possible to be discerning and confronting and to hold people accountable without being judgmental and vindictive. Acknowledgment of sin does not remove all responsibility for sin. Restitution, reform, and prevention of further wrong are required. Society has usually also attached shame and pun-

6. *Engaging the Powers* (Minneapolis: Fortress, 1992), 196-97.

ishment to wrongdoing, as is evident from the judicial system rightly holding people accountable even when they confess their guilt.

On Not Using the Bible
for Cavalier Dismissal of Wrong

Some would claim the Bible itself provides the grounds for not holding wrongdoers accountable. According to this view, if we place the focus on biblical forgiveness, then by necessity we should forgive the person and forget any idea of accountability. Two texts have been used to support this approach for Clinton. Clinton's pastor in Washington has urged leniency, as have others, by pointing to David's much worse sins of adultery with Bathsheba and intentionally putting her husband Uriah on the front lines of battle, knowing he would be killed — and declaring that David was not impeached (2 Sam 11).[7] Several people have applied the proverb "Let him who is without sin throw the first stone" (based on John 8:7). As far as I know, Matthew 18:23-35 has not been used in this debate, but this text, quite possibly *the* most significant passage on forgiveness, is also easily misused, and thus should be considered.

Anyone who points to the account of David and Bathsheba as a basis for not punishing Clinton or any other wrongdoer has either not read the text or has not paid attention to both the implicit and explicit commentary of the narrator of 2 Samuel. David's sins with Bathsheba and Uriah bring terrible grief and punishment on David's whole family. The summary description of this punishment is in 2 Samuel 12:10-11: the sword (a metaphor for killing) will never depart from his house, calamity will arise from within his house, and David's wives will be raped in broad daylight. What David did in private will be punished publicly. This alone should warn us against any thought of dividing private and public morality, as some have tried to do. Integrity is not a garment merely for public use. David confessed his sin to Nathan (12:13), but the consequences had already been set in motion.

The remainder of 2 Samuel is a narration of the resulting grief for David and his family. Three of his sons died: Amnon, Absalom, and

7. Cited by Richard Roeper, "One Thing's Certain: Clinton Is Sorry, All Right," *Chicago Sun Times* (August 18, 1998), 4.

77

Bathsheba's first child — the first two as a result of murder. David's children reenact his sins: Amnon in the rape of his sister Tamar; Absalom in the murder of Amnon and in the rape of his father's concubines.[8] Absalom seized David's kingdom in a coup, and David had to run for his life. A civil war broke out in which twenty thousand people were killed. Impeachment would have been better.

Several parts of the text bear careful reflection. King David attempted twice to cover up his sin with Bathsheba (11:6-25). Like those urging that Clinton's sin be treated lightly, David urged that his sin be treated lightly. In 11:25, after Joab, David's general, had succeeded in getting Uriah killed, David sent a message telling him not to "let this matter trouble you" [Hebrew: "be evil in your eyes"], "for the sword devours now one and now another" (NRSV translation). But in a parallelism that is lost in English translations, in 11:27 the narrator tells us that David's "matter" troubled the Lord (Hebrew: "was evil in the eyes of the Lord"). (See also 13:29, where Tamar is told not to take her rape to heart, and 13:33, where David is told not to take Amnon's death to heart.)

Strikingly, the text also shows how easily religious trappings can be subverted to cast actions in a favorable light. Absalom initiated his coup by offering sacrifices to the Lord (15:7-12). Hushai, David's spy in Absalom's court, justified his presence with Absalom with the use of religious language (16:8). But we should give David his due: in 15:24-25 he does not allow the Ark of the Covenant, the sign of God's presence, to accompany him as he flees during the coup. God would have to bring him back; he could not drag God along on his flight.

I am in no position to judge the sincerity of Clinton's use of religious language and contexts, but the danger of using religion as a self-serving device is evident. It should be obvious that no recourse should be made to the David saga as a way to justify leniency for wrongdoing, and particularly not for the wrongdoing of a leader.

More frequent recourse has been made to the statement "Let him who is without sin throw the first stone," a saying that is often used as a get-out-of-jail-free card to prevent wrongdoers from being subjected to scrutiny or punishment. The maneuver is often effective because all of us are aware of our own moral frailties and imperfec-

---

8. See J. Cheryl Exum, *Plotted, Shot, and Painted: Cultural Representations of Biblical Women* (Sheffield: Sheffield Academic Press, 1996), 21.

tions, and appropriately so. However, the use of this biblical text to avoid responsibility for sin is irresponsible and illegitimate. In this passage, a woman who has been caught in the act of adultery is brought to Jesus by the scribes and Pharisees. They remind Jesus that the law of Moses demands that such a person be killed,[9] and they then ask him what he says should be done. The narrator explicitly says that this is an attempt to test Jesus, to trap him, so that these enemies would have a basis for a charge against him. How this was a trap the narrator does not specifically explain, but almost certainly the trap is based on the fact that the occupying Roman authorities did not permit capital punishment to be administered by anyone other than themselves. The trap was an attempt to corner Jesus between the Mosaic law and the Roman authorities, something like the attempt to trap him with the question whether taxes should be paid to Caesar (Mark 12:13-17 and parallels). If Jesus were to urge leniency, he could be accused of violating the Torah; if he were to urge adherence to Torah's command, he could be brought before the Roman authorities. Therefore, Jesus' answer is an effort to avoid a trap and does not intend to teach how one should respond to evil.

But there is a much more important reason why one should not appeal to this text: *it does not belong to the original text of John's gospel.* John 7:53–8:11 has been added at some later date. As both conservative and liberal scholars know, the earliest and better manuscripts of John do not have this passage at all, and a number of other manuscripts that include the passage place a mark in the margin to indicate awareness of the textual problem. Some manuscripts have this account at the *end* of John's gospel,[10] some at Luke 21:38, one at John 7:36, and some at 7:44. Even everyday readers of English translations would know that this material does not belong to the fourth Gospel if they were paying attention to the footnotes most Bibles provide.

While it cannot be proven, this story is in all probability a piece of oral tradition that has been inserted later into the text. Indeed, I think it probably records an authentic incident from the life of Jesus, also unprovable. Whether the text should be considered canonical and authoritative is debatable, but at the very least a text like this should be used

---

9. Lev. 20:10; Deut. 22:22.

10. As indeed the first edition of the United Bible Societies' Greek New Testament does.

with the greatest caution.[11] Personally, I do not think we should form guidelines for responding to wrongdoing from this text. If the text is Jesus' response to a trap and also of dubious origin, it certainly should not be used as a quick response to avoid responsibility for sin. People must at least slow down and consider what they are doing with this text and why.

Matthew 18:23-35, the Parable of the Unforgiving Servant, deserves to be brought into this discussion, for it is a text that insists on the *necessity* of forgiveness, a forgiveness modeled on God's own forgiveness (v. 33). Christians are to be an inherently forgiving people — a point that cannot be qualified. Forgiveness, however, does not mean inattention to the responsibility for doing right, as the parable itself shows. The servant loses forgiveness because the forgiveness granted effected no change in him. Forgiveness from God *requires* change and right action.

This parable does not appear in isolation; it is part of a larger context that seeks to guide response to wrongdoing. Note how the passage unfolds:

18:3-4 emphasizes conversion and humility.[12]

18:6-9 gives a dire warning to those who cause others to do wrong and emphasizes the seriousness of wrongdoing.

18:10-14, the Parable of the Lost (Erring) Sheep, shows that God's will is that none of his "little ones" should be lost.

18:15-20 provides directions for confronting an erring brother or sister.

18:21-22 prohibits boundaries being set to limit forgiveness.

18:23-35, the Parable of the Unforgiving Servant, insists that forgiven people show forgiveness to others.

Although brief, the material on confronting a wrongdoer in 18:15-20 is the central concern, but the material preceding and following serves as a buffer to show the attitudes necessary when confronting. Reproof and forgiveness are not antithetical, and moral demands are

11. The similar problem of the ending of the Gospel of Mark (16:9-20) should be considered. Many are quick to jettison the ending of Mark, and understandably so, but by what standard — other than the fact that we like the story — do we retain John 7:53–8:11?

12. "Becoming like children" is parallel to the idea of rebirth in John 3:3-8.

not ignored. Both reproof and forgiveness are required.[13] What is involved in reproof is not detailed, but given the focus of the whole Gospel on obedience to the will of God, surely no dismissive approach to wrong is thinkable.

We may feel that forgiving and holding someone accountable at the same time is impossible, but these two acts actually deal with two separate realities. Forgiveness is primarily about one's own attitude toward the offender; holding accountable has to do with the attitude and future of the offender. (If only someone had held Clinton accountable thirty years ago!) Forgiveness is the surrender of malice and revenge in order neither to damage one's own being nor to close off avenues for the well-being, the best good, of the wrongdoer (and the good of the society). Forgiveness requires that we surrender any personal stake, any demand for retribution, any demand for seeing that our rights or any sense of justice due us are met; but if forgiveness does not at the same time seek that the offender respond with integrity to his or her own offense, *it is not Christian*. Forgiveness does not forget its moral sensitivities, for to surrender moral sensitivities is itself immoral. Forgiveness involves overcoming our attachment to ourselves,[14] and so does taking morality seriously.

This may well be the heart of the matter: our attachment to our own self-interest. The ease with which we grant forgiveness or assign condemnation often depends on our relationship to the offender and the degree to which the immoral act has affected us. We forgive most quickly those like us whose offense does not directly touch us; we condemn most quickly those unlike us, those with whom we already disagree, and those whose offense directly damages us or our interests. If Clinton had wronged our own daughter, we would not treat the matter lightly. But, for those who care at all about how society functions, is moral condemnation allowed only when we are personally violated? Have we arrived at the point that we do not care about injustice if it does not affect us personally? Does not integrity require that we evalu-

---

13. See the helpful treatment of this text by W. D. Davies and Dale C. Allison, *A Critical and Exegetical Commentary on the Gospel According to Saint Matthew* (Edinburgh: T. & T. Clark, 1991), II, 750-51 and 791-807.

14. See Michael Murray, "Repentance and Forgiveness," *The World of Forgiveness*, II.2 (1998), 19, who warns that [unthinking] forgiveness can itself foster wrongdoing. This small journal contributed significantly to my thinking about forgiveness.

ate wrongdoing in terms of truth and justice rather than in terms of self-interest? If not, we are not much different from Serbian President Slobodan Milosevic.

To What End?

Most important of all, and this has been my concern from the beginning, is the effect that our action or inaction has on strengthening or weakening moral perception in our society, a society that is obviously losing its awareness of morality. Opinion polls say that Clinton is doing a good job as a president; but by almost the same percentage, Americans say that he is unacceptable as a role model for children.[15] That is a non sequitur. Although his administration has accomplished a great deal, Clinton cannot be doing a good job if his actions lead to further deterioration of this society's morality.

I do not profess to know what should be done with Bill Clinton. Impeachment is unlikely and probably unwarranted. Resignation would be honorable, or at least would have been honorable; too much time has now transpired. Censure is certainly appropriate from a moral standpoint, but it may be questionable constitutionally and may set a dangerous precedent. If the censure course is selected, Jonathan Alter's suggestion that Clinton be required to hear the censure debate and the formal reading of the censure would seem to be a minimum.[16]

What we need is a response that can be labeled honorable. That may be difficult in the dishonorable bipartisan atmosphere we have, but it is not impossible. We could start with a national day of grieving, including a prohibition on news coverage of the event. Better than anything Congress might do would be a self-imposed punishment by Clinton himself, possibly a confinement to the White House except when absolutely necessary to govern. The Clinton White House is best known for damage control and counterattack. The President needs to change that. He needs to find a way to avoid leaving a negative moral legacy in the final years of his administration.

We cannot simply say that all leaders are corrupt. I refuse to believe that corrupt leaders are a necessary ingredient for society. If we

15. See *Newsweek* (Sept. 21, 1998), 34.
16. "Shaming the Shameless," *Newsweek* (Sept. 28, 1998) 47.

think we must have corrupt leaders to govern a corrupt world, we do not deserve to govern.[17] Two questions remain before us: Are ideals worth having and maintaining? Can a discussion take place without partisan posturing? With the convictions that morality matters and bad behavior has consequences, I want to answer yes to both questions.

---

17. See Diogenes Laertius, *Lives of Eminent Philosophers,* Antisthenes, 6.5-6 (446-366 B.C.): "States are doomed when they are unable to distinguish good men from bad. . . . It is strange that we weed out the darnel from the corn and the unfit in war, but do not excuse evil men from the service of the state."

A Biblical Perspective on the Forgiveness Debate

TROY W. MARTIN

President Clinton's "inappropriate relationships" with certain women and his subsequent requests for forgiveness have provoked a national debate on forgiveness. Participants in this debate frequently quote or allude to the adage "Forgive and forget . . . let bygones be bygones" as the guiding Christian maxim in situations of forgiveness.[1] This adage, however, does not occur in the Christian Scriptures and omits several

---

1. This adage does not occur in Christian Scripture. According to John Bartlett, the first portion of it originated with John Heywood, who wrote, "All our great fray . . . is forgiven and forgotten between us quite" (*Proverbs* [1546], 2.3; cited in *Familiar Quotations,* ed. John Bartlett, 16th edition [Boston: Little, Brown and Co., 1992], 211, n. 1). Shakespeare casts the adage in the imperative mood when he writes, "Pray you now, forget and forgive" (*King Lear* 4,7.84; cited in Bartlett, *Quotations,* 211.11). Shakespeare applies the adage differently than do modern applications. In Shakespeare's play, King Lear is the offender and uses the adage to request forgiveness from Cordelia. The adage is not a requirement placed upon the offended. P. A. Motteux uses the adage in his translation of Cervantes' *Don Quixote* 4.3.254. He translates Don Quixote's statement to Sancho as "Let us forget and forgive injuries" (P. A. Motteux, trans., *Don Quixote* [Edinburgh: John Grant, 1910], 67). However, the Spanish text reads, "Echemos pelilos a la mar." This is a Spanish proverb that translates literally as "Let us throw small hairs into the sea." Again, the offender in Motteux's translation uses the adage to seek reconciliation with the offended. Thus the adage has a different context and hence a different force than it receives in modern use.

84

essential aspects of forgiveness expressed in Scripture. First, confronting and holding the offender accountable precede forgiveness. Second, forgiveness is inextricably linked to genuine repentance. Third, responsibility for the forgiveness of an unrepentant offender should be transferred to God. Each of these aspects of forgiveness requires elaboration in view of the current debate on forgiveness.

Confrontation and Accountability

In Matthew 18:15-17, Jesus prescribes the appropriate response toward an offender. He states, "If your brother sins [against you], go and tell him his fault between you and him alone" (Matt. 18:15a, New American Bible). In contrast to the forgive-and-forget prescription, Jesus prescribes confrontation, not forgiveness, as the appropriate initial response. If the offender remains obstinate, more and more members of the community are to be brought into the confrontation to hold the transgressor accountable (Matt. 18:16-17). In this passage Jesus clearly prescribes confrontation and accountability before forgiveness of the offender occurs.

Not only does Jesus prescribe this response, he practices it. Jesus summons his generation to repent (Matt. 4:17). He confronts the Pharisees and scribes with their hypocrisy (Matt. 5:20; 6:2, 5, 16; 9:3-6, 11-13; 12:2-8, 10-14, 24-32, 33-37, 38-42; 15:1-14; 16:1-4; 19:8; 21:45-46; 22:15-22; 23:1-12, 13-36), the Sadducees with their error (21:12-17, 23-27, 45-46; 22:23-32), the citizens of Nazareth with their shame (13:54-58), and his disciples with their lack of faith (6:21, 31; 8:26; 14:31; 16:23; 17:17-20). Jesus predicts stern judgment for the unrepentant (10:14-15, 33, 37-39; 11:16-19, 20-24; 23:13-36) rather than following the forgive-and-forget formula.

The early church imitated Jesus in confronting and holding the guilty accountable. According to Acts, Peter repeatedly confronts the crowds in Jerusalem for killing Jesus (Acts 2:23, 36; 3:13-15) and summons them to repent (Acts 2:38; 3:19). Stephen's similar confrontation with those responsible for Jesus' death results in his own martyrdom (Acts 7:51-60). Peter confronts Ananias and Sapphira with their deed (Acts 5:1-11). Peter and John confront the baptized Simon with his evil intentions and demand that he repent (Acts 8:20-24). Paul and Barnabas vociferously challenge the discriminatory actions of Christian

Pharisees (Acts 15:1-2). Paul writes to the Galatians that he has had to correct Peter for similar discrimination toward the Gentiles. Following Jesus' teaching and example, the early church practices confrontation and accountability instead of the cheap, easy forgiveness encouraged by the forgive-and-forget adage.

In the current debate on forgiveness, some contend that those who confront President Clinton violate Jesus' command "Judge not lest you be judged" (Matt. 7:1; Luke 6:37). This commandment does not, however, preclude recognition of or confrontation with the faults of others. Jesus explains this commandment by prescribing, "Remove the wooden beam from your eye first; then you will see clearly to remove the splinter from your brother's eye" (Matt. 7:5-6). Those who confront President Clinton and attempt "to remove the splinter" are practicing rather than violating Jesus' teaching on forgiveness as prescribed in the Gospels. The public dimension of this confrontation indicates that the private dimension was either absent or ineffective. Nevertheless, the public dimension has elicited a request for forgiveness from President Clinton, and this request raises a second aspect of forgiveness expressed in the New Testament.

Genuine Repentance, the Prerequisite for Forgiveness

In addition to its insistence on confrontation and accountability, the New Testament also insists that genuine repentance is a prerequisite for forgiveness. In Mattew 18:15-18, Jesus says a repentant sinner should be forgiven. However, he emphasizes that a recalcitrant transgressor should be expelled, not forgiven (Matt. 18:16-17). Jesus then bequeaths to his church the authority not to forgive the unrepentant (i.e., "to bind") as well as to forgive the repentant (i.e., "to loose") (Matt. 18:18). The Parable of the Unforgiving Servant, which immediately follows, emphasizes the necessity of genuine repentance before forgiveness is extended. In this familiar parable, Jesus tells of a debtor who owes his master ten thousand talents, which Jesus describes as "a huge amount." Actually, a talent represents six thousand drachmas, and a single drachma is a customary day's wage for workers. This debtor is sixty million days' wages in debt. Jesus' understatement that "he had no way of paying it back" probably brought a smile to the faces in his audience. This smile likely turned into a burst of laughter when the debtor implores his master, "Be patient with me, and I will pay you back in full." The posture of the debtor — falling down and doing homage to his master, as well as owning responsibility for the debt — elicits compassion from this master, who immediately forgives the entire amount! Later, however, this "forgiven" debtor finds another who owes him one hundred days' worth of drachmas and demands that he pay up (Matt. 18:28). Disregarding this person's entreaty for leniency, the "forgiven" debtor delivers him up to prison (Matt. 18:30). These actions demonstrate to the master that the "forgiven" debtor's posture and words did not represent genuine repentance. Consequently, the master recalls the "forgiven" debtor and reinstates the entire original debt (Matt. 18:34). Jesus' parable demonstrates that genuine repentance is absolutely necessary for forgiveness. Even in a case where forgiveness is already extended, forgiveness may be revoked if the injured party discovers that the transgressor made a show of repentance devoid of genuine contrition.

In addition to this parable, Colossians 3:13 and Ephesians 4:32 advocate genuine repentance as a necessary prerequisite for forgiveness. In both, the Lord's forgiveness serves as the paradigm for his followers' forgiveness. Colossians 3:13b reads: "As the Lord has forgiven you, so must you also do." Ephesians 4:32b reads: "Forgiving one another as God has forgiven you in Christ." Throughout the New Testament, the announcement of God's forgiveness is preceded by a call for repentance. If a sinner's repentance is a prerequisite for the Lord's extending forgiveness and the Lord's forgiveness is a paradigm for Christian forgiveness, then genuine repentance is also a necessary prerequisite for the forgiveness of a transgressor.

President Clinton's request for forgiveness raises the issue of what constitutes genuine repentance. Many mention his tone of voice and physical appearance as evidence of his sincerity. Even though these characteristics are important, the decisive proof of true repentance is action. In Acts, Paul summarizes his message by saying, "I preached the need to repent and turn to God, and to do works giving evidence of repentance" (Acts 26:20). The Philippian jailer demonstrates his repentance by tending the wounds of his prisoners and feeding them (Acts 16:33). A repentant Zacchaeus states, "Behold, half of my possessions, Lord, I shall give to the poor, and if I have extorted anything from anyone I shall repay it four times over" (Luke 19:8). Salvation would never have come to Zacchaeus's house if he were to have said, "I am sorry, and I am instructing my legal counsel to mount a vigorous defense against my accusers." Genuine repentance results in action that seeks to right the wrong as much as possible. For many, President Clinton's actions following his request for forgiveness do not evidence of genuine repentance. This situation raises a third aspect of forgiveness expressed in the New Testament.

Transferring Responsibility for Forgiveness to God

When Jesus' generation finally crucified him, his death prohibited him from holding his contemporaries accountable any longer. But just before he died, Jesus prayed, "Father, forgive them; for they know not what they do" (Luke 23:34). At first glance, these words appear to sanction the forgive-and-forget formula even when offenders remain unrepentant. After all, Jesus prays for the forgiveness of his tormentors even while they are crucifying him. His prayer certainly reveals his willingness to forgive. Nevertheless, a crucial distinction exists between Jesus' prayer for his Father to forgive his persecutors and Jesus' own utterance of forgiveness. Jesus does not say to his persecutors, "I forgive you." Instead, he prays for God to forgive them. His prayer transfers the process of forgiveness to God. God now becomes responsible for holding these culprits accountable and for forgiving them should they repent. Since God's forgiveness is always linked to repentance, Jesus' prayer does not effect the forgiveness of these offenders.

Similarly, Stephen, prior to dying beneath a barrage of stones thrown by the crowd, prays, "Lord, do not hold this sin against them" (Acts 7:60). He does not say, "I forgive you"; instead, he transfers the responsibility of forgiveness to the Lord. And sometime later, Saul, one of the participants in Stephen's murder, is accosted on the Damascus Road by the Lord, who does not proclaim forgiveness for Saul, but says, "Saul, Saul, why are you persecuting me?" (Acts 9:4) Saul's forgiveness is inextricably linked to his repentant attitude, demonstrated by his three-day fast (Acts 9:9). Were he to have remained recalcitrant, it is unlikely he would have survived his Damascus Road experience. The example of Saul demonstrates that Stephen's dying prayer does not effect the forgiveness of his persecutors but transfers the responsibility of forgiving to the Lord when Stephen is no longer able to hold his tormentors accountable.

The New Testament insightfully recognizes the importance of this response toward an unrepentant offender for preserving the well-being of the victim. Continued contact between the offended and an unresponsive offender often results in feelings of resentment, bitterness, and hatred. When a victim has exhausted every means of holding a perpetrator accountable, the victim should transfer responsibility for the recalcitrant perpetrator to God. This transference provides emotional, psychological, and spiritual freedom to the offended even while the unresolved relationship with the offender remains.

In contrast to the forgive-and-forget adage, this transference does not require those harmed by President Clinton's actions to exonerate him if, in their opinion, he fails to demonstrate genuine repentance by his actions. By transferring the responsibility of forgiveness to God, they are able to recognize the continued injustice of the situation and yet be freed emotionally, psychologically, and spiritually from the responsibility of making it right. By this transference, the New Testament provides for their well-being in the face of an unresponsive offender, who may still face legal, constitutional, or eschatological consequences for his actions.

Conclusion

The forgive-and-forget adage is not adequate to inform our understanding of forgiveness in the current national debate. In particular, this adage does not comprehend the necessity of confronting and holding an offender accountable. It does not encompass genuine repentance as a necessary prerequisite for forgiveness, nor does it envision transferring responsibility for an unrepentant offender to God. In all these respects, the New Testament understanding of forgiveness transcends the adage and more appropriately responds to issues raised in the current debate.

African-American Pastoral Theology as Public Theology: The Crisis of Private and Public in the White House

EDWARD P. WIMBERLY

African-Americans in the church overwhelmingly support President Bill Clinton in his present moral crisis. Some who are disturbed by this are asking why and searching for an explanation for this unquestioned loyalty. Why African-American Christians give almost unanimous backing to President Clinton is the reason for this brief essay. My explanation is that the President shares a small-town, folksy, rural style with black preachers and Southern white politicians. Such a style, when used by an attractive, gifted, and charismatic figure, resonates at a deep level with African-American Christians, especially when that figure — notably a preacher/politician — articulates some of the central values to which African-Americans adhere.

As indicated, one of the characteristics of the Southern folk style of leadership is captured in the ability of the preacher/politician to articulate the cherished values deeply embedded in the unconscious as well as the conscious mind. The preacher/politician who articulates these values using a combination of metaphors, images, and word pictures reaches the very souls of African-Americans. Characteristically, they elevate a person with this gift of communication, whether preacher or politician, to the status of a biblical prophet, especially as personified by Moses. Moreover, they assign to such communicative persons special status, and they separate their character and personal life from their gifts. Because of their gifts, these talented communicators become exempt from the normal expectations of morality and from the normal rules to which persons without such gifts would be expected to adhere. One of the contemporary examples of this status is the gifted athlete who is exempted from normal expectations of morality because of his or her extraordinary athletic prowess. The personal and private life of the gifted athlete or the master communicator is off limits; thus, sexual indiscretions and other moral lapses are automatically excused.

One of the basic questions I have had to ask myself, as an African-American ordained minister, is whether, in the long run, African-Americans are well served by such gifted people. Does it really matter whether or not there is consistency and congruence between the preacher/politician's private life and his or her public life? Does it really make a difference whether a preacher/politician has a "correct" political agenda but behaves outrageously in his or her private life? In my mind, the answers to these questions depend on the kinds of expectations we as African-American Christians have of such persons.

The results of the 1998 elections on November 3 reveal that the economy was the dominant factor in voters' maintaining the political status quo in the United States Senate and increasing the number of Democrats in the House of Representatives. People's expectations obviously were related to the material and social benefits of not only a good economy but also the current balance of power. For African-Americans, economic benefits were important considerations, as were continued opportunities to have cherished cultural values articulated in the White House. An added benefit is the joy that comes from seeing our most respected people of color associated with people in high places. But, benefits notwithstanding, the question is, should these rewards and satisfactions be all that we expect? Is there anything more that we should demand from the preacher/politicians who court our allegiance?

As an African-American minister, I think we need to expect more from our leaders than merely their gift of gab, their name recognition, and the material satisfaction we experience because of their domestic policies. I believe that personal character and public policy go hand in hand. We need leaders who can "walk the walk" as well as "talk the talk." More precisely, African-Americans need leaders who do not engage in self-destructive and self-sabotaging behaviors that make them a political liability. If a preacher/politician is known to have personal practices and habits that might hurt him or her and lead to removal from office, we should avoid electing that person to office. It is reasonable to expect that our leaders would have the personal maturity and integrity to behave in ways consistent with their office. Too much is at stake for the preacher/politician to engage in private activities that compromise truth and integrity.

I agree with Stephen L. Carter, who helps us look at the integrity of life and political action. As an African-American best-selling author and lawyer, Carter reminds us that

> the word *integrity* comes from the same Latin root as *integer* and historically has been understood to carry much the same sense, the sense of wholeness: a person of integrity, like a whole number, is a whole person, a person somehow undivided. The word conveys not so much a single-mindedness as a completeness; not the frenzy of a fanatic who wants to remake all the world in a single mold but the serenity of a person who is confident in the knowledge that he or she is living rightly. The person of integrity need not be a Gandhi but also cannot be a person who blows up buildings to make a point. A person of integrity lurks somewhere inside each of us: a person we feel we can trust to do right, to play by the rules, to keep commitments.[1]

Carter also reminds us that religion teaches that living is a call to integrity, completeness, and wholeness.[2] He calls us to remember that Western culture tried to find in Christianity a guide for the well-lived life. It seems to me that we have forgotten that the good life is not just one of economic and material well-being, but is a whole life of integrity in which honesty, fidelity, compassion, commitment, forthrightness, steadfastness, and consistency are paramount. While integrity at all levels of life is a lofty and elusive goal, moral and political leadership demands that we respect it and not play with it. One important example of not respecting it and playing with it would be lying under oath.

The point is that the pursuit of integrity means that it is impossible to separate life into discrete segments. The way life is put together de-

---

1. Stephen L. Carter, *Integrity* (New York: Basic Books, 1996), 7.
2. Ibid., 8.

mands that we view it as an integral whole. To separate private from public distorts the way life should be lived. It is also impossible to separate private life from public life when the well-being of others is dependent on the actions of the preacher/politician. How many people will suffer needlessly if a political figure in whom they trust and hope is removed from office because of morally reprehensible private behavior?

I want to put forward a case for integrity in the private and public life of politicians based on what I have learned as a minister who is both a pastoral counselor and a pastoral theologian. As a pastoral counselor, I get realistic glimpses into how the lack of integrity in one's personal life impacts the growth and development of others. I believe that people suffer dire consequences when their leaders choose not to pursue integrity. One of the major results of the loss of integrity among our leaders is the difficulty in inspiring trust, which is essential for the security people need to grow and develop. A lack of integrity frustrates our growth and impedes our ability to form healthy communities.

A Pastoral Theological Point of View

I speak not only as an African-American, but also as an African-American pastoral theologian. A pastoral theologian is one who reflects on the practice of pastoral care and counseling and draws insights that can be used to clarify theological and practical issues. Normally, pastoral theologians are concerned with personal, family, extended family, and small community network issues. However, a concern for wholeness means that we must also attend to much broader issues. What the pastoral theologian offers is insights into such public issues as justice, forgiveness, sexual harassment, infidelity, compassion, and human sexuality. These issues take on new meaning when a pastoral theologian brings to bear on them insights from what he or she has learned through pastoral counseling. In essence, what the pastoral theologian does is reflect on the practice of pastoral counseling, using both theological and psychological perspectives to generate knowledge and information that can be used to help those who are in counseling and to help clarify important public issues. In this sense, a pastoral theologian becomes a public theologian.

What is significant about the practice of pastoral counseling is that it is possible to glean a depth perspective on those who engage in what I call destructive and risky behavior similar to that engaged in by Monica Lewinsky and President Clinton. While forgiveness and justice are obvious concerns, the pastoral theologian is also interested in the phenomenological experiences of those who are impacted by a lack of integrity in our public leaders. Phenomenologically, the question is, What can be learned from those who are innocent victims when public leaders behave immorally? Another question is, What can be learned from those who habitually engage in acts that compromise the lives of others? In the context of wholeness and integrity, was the behavior of President Clinton and Moncia Lewinsky completely harmless in its impact? Was their behavior solely a private matter and a problem only for the first family?

What I have learned about irresponsible adult sexual behavior is that its harmfulness extends beyond the people directly involved. Such behavior encompasses a wider circle and touches people in ways that lessen their self-esteem and lower their level of trust in the basic institutions needed for growth, development, and fulfillment. Moreover, those who are adversely affected by this irresponsible behavior may lose confidence in their own ability to live lives of integrity. Pastoral counseling has taught me that integrated people are key to developing institutions of integrity. People and institutions of integrity are essential for developing valued and contributing human beings. Our welfare as individuals, families, communities, states, and a nation is impacted by the personal and private behavior of our leaders. Integrity demands that we see life as a congruent whole with interacting and interpenetrating facets.

Trust is the foundation of our private and public institutional life. Pastoral counseling has taught me that when trust is broken by the conduct of respected leaders, its restoration is a long and difficult process. While people can be forgiven, the level of trust they once had is difficult, and sometimes impossible, to reestablish. The process of reconciliation following a breach of trust is mysterious and painful, and the outcome cannot be predicted. Moreover, those who betray a trust may not be able to deal with the anger and hurt of those whose trust has been betrayed. The point is that the shallow manner in which President Clinton handled his own confession has done very little to restore trust in him or his leadership. Those of us who understand the reconciliation process must not only forgive; we must also point out the cost of reconciliation. We need to take the reconciliation process seriously because irreparable damage may have already been done.

In pastoral counseling I have encountered some concrete problems among African-Americans that shed light on the topic at hand. One is the problem of "settling," and the other is the problem of overcoming trust betrayed during early childhood.

The Problem of "Settling"

Among African-American women there is a popular concept called "settling." Settling occurs when a woman lowers her expectations of a man in order to secure male companionship. The objective is to find intimate companionship. Many African-American women indicate that settling is one of the most self-destructive behaviors in which women can engage. Some conclude that women are better off remaining alone than settling for less than they deserve. One of the best explanations of settling comes from the work of Renita Weems, an African-American biblical scholar at Vanderbilt University, in her book *I Asked for Intimacy*.[3] Her work on the Leah Syndrome seems to capture what I have learned from African-American women counselees about the impact on them of a lack of integrity. Leah, described in the twenty-ninth chapter of the book of Genesis, is a woman who waited around for a man who did not want her. For Weems, the Leah Syndrome is about women who love too much, who conspire against themselves, who use their sexuality to snare men they would be better off without, who get into relationships that destroy them, and who "settle" when they could do better.[4] She does not see these women as victims; she sees them as relationship addicts. Relationship addicts are those who tie their self-esteem to others rather than find it within themselves and in their relationship with God.[5] Such women, she says, settle for any kind of relationship when no relationship at all might be better for their self-esteem.

There is an analogy between the Leah Syndrome and the political behavior of many African-Americans. This analogy fits the problems we see with our President and the African-Americans who "settle" for

---

3. Renita J. Weems, *I Asked for Intimacy: Stories of Blessings, Betrayals, and Birthings* (San Diego: LuraMedia, 1993).

4. Ibid., 62-63.

5. Ibid.

leaders who cannot, in their private and public behavior, meet our expectations. Settling, then, is hazardous to the political well-being of African-Americans. We would be better off without such leaders. African-Americans are working overtime to keep President Clinton in
office, fearing that his downfall would be ours as well. Are those who
are critical of settling correct?

As African-Americans, and certainly as voters, we are being taken
for granted. Settling reinforces our low self-esteem and drives us
deeper into dependency upon others for our survival. Our future
should be based on integrity and the pursuit of wholeness in every facet
of life, not on the results of a political election. We should not be reduced to being political junkies looking for a fix in the promises of
those who seek to manipulate and misuse our votes.

The Coming Alive of Black Men

In counseling I have been seeing more and more black men who are de-
ciding to make a difference in the lives of their families and communities, even though their own lives were complicated by a loss of trust in
key adults when they were children. These men have long histories of
broken promises, particularly from adult men in their lives. Many of
these men, now in their mid-thirties and beyond, are recognizing that
through religious faith and commitment they can make a difference in
their own lives and the lives of those they love, as well as in their communities. They are learning to overcome the obstacles and limitations
imposed by their upbringing.

Pastoral counseling is one way they are seeking to put a life of integrity together, but it is not the only way. As I have indicated, religious
faith and involvement in community service are helping to make the
difference. Whatever resources these men have lacked from without,
they are finding from within — within themselves, within their stories,
and within their increased involvement in religious and community activities. The major difference I see is that these men have decided that
they will no longer be victims of the system.

What I have learned from these men is that they spent the first
part of their lives looking outside themselves for answers to life's problems. They felt that the responsibility for their well-being rested elsewhere. As a result, they developed an irresponsible dependency rather

than an interdependency through which they could contribute to the growth and development of others, as others contributed to theirs. Black men in counseling are beginning to look beyond their deficits to their strengths. They are forming covenants with those who can help them develop these strengths. Like the women who are refusing to settle, these men are also recognizing that many of the solutions to their problems are in a realistic appraisal of their strengths, setting realistic goals, an involvement in religious and spiritual pursuits, a sense of service to community, and less reliance on others for what they can do themselves.

As African-Americans, we can learn from what I see occurring in pastoral counseling with both black women and men. Our future as a whole people is in our own hands, and it begins with our religious and spiritual roots. It then branches out into other dimensions of our lives. Indeed, our salvation is in the pursuit of a whole life, a life of integrity, one balanced among spiritual, relational, recreational, nutritional, service, political, and economic endeavors. To place all our hope in a political solution exacerbates our problems and lowers our collective self-esteem.

Conclusion

Pastoral theology helps us to discern the connection between the public and private dimensions of our lives. Moreover, it helps us to recognize the importance of integrity as wholeness and undividedness. Indeed, one of the positive dimensions of postmodernism is a rediscovery of the holistic dimension of our existence. We are no longer victims of the Cartesian and Enlightenment compartmentalization of life. We are integral human beings living in integral communities. The concept of a global village is not simply a convenient political catchword; it is basic to the nature of our lived life.

Finally, as African-Americans, we need to put as much faith in our own selves and our own communities as we put in President Clinton and the federal government. Relying too heavily on a politician for our well-being is dangerous, given the rapidity of political change. We need a more consistent means, in addition to that offered by the government, to continue economic and social development. For example, when "welfare as we know it" changes, thousands of people, not just African-Americans, will have to make significant adjustments in their lives. Some major shifts in what we have expected from the government will need to occur.

The point in all of this is that the private life of the preacher/politician cannot be kept separate from his or her public life. Risky private behavior makes him or her vulnerable to the whims of political gaming. Private misbehavior by the preacher/politician will not only bring him or her down, but will also affect all those who depend on that person. It is far too simplistic to say that the private life of the preacher/politician does not matter.

Theologically, African-American Christians have always trusted in the righteousness of God — a God who always keeps promises even when God's timing of fulfillment differs from our own. We also see Jesus as a righteous man, a person of integrity whom we should emulate. Would it be too much to expect that the preacher/politician who constantly appeals to religious values would not only espouse these values but also attempt to live them out in private and in public? Those of us who comprise the church in the African-American experience need to upgrade our standards and expectations for those who seek our vote. God wants more for us than empty promises.

Christian Doctrine and
Presidential Decisions

GABRIEL FACKRE

The presidential crisis poses questions long discussed in Christian theology: sin and forgiveness, private faith and public order, human nature and its possibilities all have to do with the classical Christian doctrines of soteriology, Christology, anthropology, and more. Ancient debates on the relationship of justification to sanctification, the "two kingdoms theory" and the sovereignty of Christ, and the relationship of the soul to society reappear in these current controversies. Historic theological traditions, while not often identified as such, assert themselves in opinions fervently held — Baptist, Methodist, Reformed, Lutheran, Roman Catholic, and so forth.

An interesting thing about the signatories to the "Declaration concerning Religion, Ethics, and the Crisis in the Clinton Presidency" is the diversity of doctrinal traditions represented. What accounts for the convergence? One possibility is the attempt to draw on a common stock of classical premises while at the same time deploying the insights of one's own heritage. What follows is a self-conscious effort to draw on both the commonalities and diversities of classical teaching. Of course, a straight line cannot be drawn from doctrine to political decisions. Many with similar commitments have come to different conclusions. Yet people of faith must make the connection between their deepest convictions and their life in the *polis*.

The presidential crisis is multidimensional; its varied aspects are distinguishable but not separable. The Declaration is an attempt to recognize the differences among religious, moral, functional, and legal considerations but to declare for their inseparability. This dialectic has warrants in a classical Christian understanding of human nature and related distinguishable-but-inseparable refrains in Christian doctrine.[1]

Human beings live "at the juncture of nature and spirit," finite yet free, as Reinhold Niebuhr notably expressed it.[2] We are enmeshed in the "contingencies and necessities" of bodily existence with its biological and social matrices, which constitute our "creatureliness." At the same time, the self so shaped by these relationships is able to discern, and, in turn, affect them. Freedom-within-finitude is part of what the Christian tradition identifies as "the image of God."[3] The self in its capacity to choose, affected though not determined by our spatial-temporal rootedness, is accountable to its Maker through the twofold commandment to love God and neighbor.

And who can fulfill the radical double imperative? "No one living is righteous before you" (Ps. 143:2). So we confess our common sin and look to the mercy of God. And the church reflects on their meaning in its doctrines of the Fall and the Work of Christ. But "commandment" functions not only as judgment descending on a universal propensity, but also as a guide for particular decisions. Thus the Decalogue with the second table's "thou shalt nots" presupposes our distorted state and translates the two counsels of heavenly perfection into earthly norms, realizable albeit imperfectly.

Both the radical love ethic, with its judgment on all of us, and the Decalogue's seventh and ninth commandments have a bearing on the issues at hand. Our common rebel state, exposed by the imperatives of *agape,* demands a self-critical humility when assessing the President's behavior. Yet a simplistic "they/we all do it" is fatal to the purposes of

---

1. "Distinguishable but inseparable" is a refrain in Christian doctrine. It appears in Christology as the distinct divine and human natures inseparable in the one Person; the Trinity as distinguishable Persons coinherent in the one Being of God; in ecclesiology as the Body of Christ inseparable from a body of people; in sacramentology as the eucharistic real Presence in and with ordinary elements and actions, etc.

2. Developed in detail in *The Nature and Destiny of Man,* vols. I and II (New York: Charles Scribner's Sons, 1948).

3. The *imago Dei* has other dimensions, including its human-divine and human-human interrelationships.

the Decalogue. A breach of these standards is a serious matter of particulars that goes beyond Sunday's general confession of sin

The "Religious" Dimension

The President's various public professions of sin are an acknowledgment of his accountability to specific standards of fidelity and truth telling. This is especially true of the letter he sent to his Southern Baptist congregation, which puts the matter squarely in a Christian context. This uniquely *religious* dimension of "repentance" sends us to the New Testament understanding of *metanoia:* it has to do with an "about-face," like that of a prodigal who turns around and makes his way back home with penitent heart and confessional word. Reflecting this reversal of direction, a long tradition in the church construes repentance as a threefold movement: contrition of the heart, confession of the mouth, and satisfaction by hands and feet.[4] The last is the visible sign of a turnaround, the intention and effort to make amends for harm done, one that lends credence to the invisibilities of the heart and the audibilities of the mouth.

"Repentance" is the language of faith, an act done, first and fore-

---

4. Of course this is the formula for the historic Roman Catholic rite of penance. Reformation wariness about "works righteousness" should not discount the intent of the third movement, "satisfaction." Protestant liturgies of assurance of pardon and/or absolution use language similar to the Roman Catholic "purpose of amendment," as in "Penance, The Sacrament of," *A Catholic Dictionary,* Donald Atwater, ed. (New York: Macmillan, 1961), 376-77. Thus *The Book of Common Prayer* reads: "The Almighty and merciful Lord grant you absolution and remission of all your sins, true repentance, amendment of life, and the grace and consolation of the Holy Spirit" (New York: Seabury Press, 1979), 32. Likewise, the "Assurance of Pardon" of the Evangelical and Reformed Church states: "I do declare unto you, who do truly repent and heartily believe in Jesus Christ, and are sincerely determined to amend your sinful life, the forgiveness of all your sins. . . ." The remarkable new document currently under consideration, *Joint Declaration of the Catholic Church and the Lutheran World Federation on the Doctrine of Justification,* asserts a common understanding of justification in which grace is both the imputation of Christ's righteousness to sinners and the impartation of renewal — both pardon and power, albeit accented differently in the two traditions. The Protestant stress on a forensic forgiveness too often flirts with antinomianism and must be reminded by a Bonhoeffer that, while grace is free, it is not cheap. Hence his paradox: "Only those who believe, obey; only those who obey, believe."

101

most, *coram Deo,* not to be confused with apologies made to offended parties nor taken to erase political or moral consequences. While having a distinguishable integrity of its own, this "vertical" relationship is not separable from life in its "horizontal" connections. Repentance is lodged in the *imago,* but it is the exercise of an accountable freedom before God with necessary entailments in creaturely relationships, in this case political ones. While the personal is not, as such, the political, it cannot be severed from the political. Contrition and confession must be completed by turnaround acts of amendment for injuries inflicted in the *polis.*

The institutional facet of presidential repentance cannot avoid facing irresponsible actions taking place in a House of the people, lies told to the people, distraction from the business of the people, and the erosion of the moral discourse of the people. Of course, the Starr pruriencies and the Republican partisanships have contributed to the present distractions and erosions. But religious repentance is marked by honest self-criticism, leaving it to others to face their God.

"But wait a minute! Aren't you courting a doctrine of salvation by works? We don't have to do anything to make God merciful! Grace is free, not earned."

Grace *is* free. The ultimate judgment on human sin is received by God on the cross of Christ, the miracle of the Judge judged. We are saved by grace alone, received by faith alone. Grace is free, but it is not *cheap.* Authentic faith is busy in costly love, obedience, and fruits meet for repentance. In the standard liturgy, the assurance of pardon is "promised in the Gospel to all who repent and believe . . . with full purpose of new obedience." In this case, no payment of the ultimate penalty on Golgotha relieves one of penultimate obediences and penalties for sins that affect the political order.

What would presidential repentance look like? It would have to include all three movements — contrition, confession, and satisfaction for injuries inflicted. The first is known only to God. The second has been made. And the third? Surely it must entail some sign given of undoing the damage done to the people's House, the upholding of its laws, distraction from its business, and the debilitation of its agenda and discourse. Those who resist resignation as an act of amendment have yet to make a case for a convincing alternative.[5]

---

5. In "Face the Music" (*New Republic,* Nov. 16, 1998, 11-12), Donald Schapiro and Robert A. Schapiro propose an arguable alternative. They hold that

The Moral Dimension

The moral dimension is yet another distinguishable but not separable aspect of the presidential crisis, one evidence being the associations with the religious dimension noted above. By "moral" I mean both internal rectitude and external behavior in conformity to it. Again, the Decalogue's second table is a working norm for both of these aspects in the Christian tradition; many hold that these standards are a moral law universally inscribed on both conscience and culture. To claim that it is obeisance to the Religious Right to press the moral case in matters political is a caricature of the first order.[6] It is also a misreading of Christian history, especially of the Reformed tradition, which insists on the regency of the same Christ over both soul and society. This passion for public accountability, however, needs to be tempered by Lutheran realism about the *simul iustus et peccator*.[7]

Moral scoundrels have certainly done things of political beneficence. Further, there is no simple division between saints and sinners in the civil order, for the ultimate norm of Jesus Christ exposes the flaws of all. Given the moral ambiguities that attend political life, we regularly must choose the lesser of evils. The moral and the political cannot be simplistically fused, as the moralist is tempted to do.

But while the moralist is wrong, so is the separatist. We return to our anthropology. What transpires in that tiny tower of freedom that rises from finitude affects those natural and social contingencies, even as it is affected by them. Over time, government — especially a democratic government that depends on the confidence of the people in its processes — cannot survive without some measure of trustworthiness in its elected leaders. A pattern of disdain for moral law in speech and

censure is too little and impeachment or forced resignation are too much. A "third option" is one in which a President "sworn to uphold the laws" would "subject himself to these laws." They urge Clinton to agree to face criminal prosecution after completing his tenure in office, accepting no pardon that would abort such procedures.

6. See the writer's early critique in *The Religious Right and Christian Faith* (Grand Rapids: Eerdmans, 1982).

7. Hence in matters both theological and political the kind of "mutual affirmation and admonition" urged by the recent Lutheran-Reformed accord in North America, set forth initially in Keith E. Nickle and Timothy F. Lull, eds., *A Common Calling: The Witness of Our Reformation Churches in North America Today* (Minneapolis: Augsburg Fortress, 1993).

behavior will have its consequences in policy and governance. So too the moral fabric of a society cannot help but become frayed by the practice of its national leader. If the President can do such and such, why not the corporation CEO, the high school teacher, and the teenager so taught? Or, in military terms, why not the sergeant as well as the commander-in-chief?

The finitude/freedom bonding works the other way as well. The bad choices and actions of a national leader are not an island separated from the moral practices of the mainland. We live today in the cultures of lying and promiscuity, as a click-on of the evening cable TV roster or an Internet search engine quickly reveals. The President is a creature of these contingencies. The social ethicist reminds us of the context of our corruptions of freedom. No indictment of the President is apt without dealing with the guilt of the powers and principalities that foster these cultures, and of us who accede to them.

Yet Presidents are not above the moral law, nor can they hide behind the ubiquity of its violation. This is especially true where the actions of an office that shapes the national ethos undercut the cultures of truth telling and fidelity. We return, therefore, to an expectation of some sign of the third movement of repentance. Both the moral and religious dimensions pose these questions to the President himself. They are not, first and foremost, matters to be decided in a political forum or congressional tribunal. While distinguishable from the latter, they are not, however, inseparable from two more dimensions that do involve these forums and tribunals: the functional and the legal.

The Functional Dimension

The functional question is whether the President can effectively execute his office given the impact of the scandal and of the impeachment inquiry. While a pragmatic consideration, it is not unrelated to the religious and moral dimensions. In the fallen world discerned by Christian anthropology, political decisions are the art of the possible and thus alert to the practicable. In terms of consequences, is it better to "move on" and away from the present inquiry in the interest of needed attention to the large issues that face the nation? Or should we press the case for resignation or impeachment because a weakened presidency can only jeopardize the nation and the very causes for which President Clinton stands?

Lending force to the first argument are data from both the professional pollster and the election polls that show continuing support for the President's political performance and the wish to put the whole matter behind us. So too the President's current successes in mediating international disputes. Thus the separationists are given aid and comfort by the pragmatists.

But here the inseparabilities must weigh in. The same religious and moral considerations that assert a place for pragmatics can make a case that there is no "moving on" and leaving behind the scandal. The widespread disillusionment with the President's personal morality will impact negatively on the effectiveness of a continuing presidency. Further, pragmatically, the alternative is not the end of the programs and policies to which the public apparently gives assent; for it is the Vice President, not their opponents, who is in the wings prepared to carry them forward. And again, one obvious way of "moving on" is for the President to withdraw from the scene, a courageous act of about-face that might well secure his otherwise commendable political legacy.

The pollsters' almost daily data-gathering plays an important part in the functionalist argument for the President to stay his present course. But here inseparable moral and religious commitments must weigh in. Christian decision-making before God can never let the givens of history constitute themselves as normative. The moral *is* cannot be the moral *ought,* as the present state is always short of the final reign of God. So in the midst of his own givens of the 1930s, Dietrich Bonhoeffer's wise counsel: do not be servile before fact. The polls presume to state our own givens. Indeed, they threaten to become our "new morality" and thus an invitation to political servility. Here too the moral/political interconnections are a factor. Poll data on moral questions cannot be separated from a culture whose conscience has not been much formed by family, school, and religious institutions. And with respect to pragmatics itself, a culture of volatility, whose views can change dramatically from one day to the next (with poll results being "snapshots of the moment"), is a poor platform for thoughtful public policy. On balance, the considerations within the functional cum religio-moral dimension add weight to the choice of resignation.

Gabriel Fackre

The Legal Dimension

Is impeachment the legal dimension of the crisis? Basic theological commitments have both indirect and direct import. Our creaturely embodiment has its institutional underside, in this case the world of governance and its laws. As the Declaration asserts, the functions of government, eminently so its highest office, require trust in professions of truth. Behind the legal talk of perjury lies the unspoken, and sometimes spoken, covenant: "I am telling the truth." In traditional Christian teaching, the need for the state, as an "order of preservation" against the disorders introduced by human perversity, presupposes the responsible ordering of speech. False witness undermines the capacity to govern.

Does the President caught in a lie rise to the level of "high crimes and misdemeanors"? Here the evidence reviewed by Congress will be decisive. If a *pattern* of lying is established, it puts into question the trustworthiness of the President in testimony he might give on any subject. How is this not a misdemeanor that imperils the office? Right now, the jury is out on the evidence for this charge. Abuse of power? Realism about the corruptibility of power in the hands of sinful humans is a basic of Christian anthropology. This sobriety about our condition found its way into the Constitution in its suspicion of pyramided power and thus its checking and balancing of executive, legislative, and judicial branches. The presidential impeachment process is one outworking of this Lord Acton–like sensibility. "Abuse of power" in that context would have to entail evidence of the imbalancing of power vis-à-vis the other branches of government or an agglomeration deleterious to the country. While the abuse of personal power in the relationship of the President to a powerless intern is morally outrageous, it does not appear to qualify in the latter terms. Again, a pattern of abuse of the office must be established for it to rise to the stipulated standards of impeachment.

One direct implication of Christian doctrinal premises that keeps company with these indirect connections has to do with the possible role of poll morality in the impeachment process. Congressional servility before the polls — one way or the other — would match the President's own seductions by sexual givens.

Decisions on the presidential crisis need to take into account the particularities and interweavings of these religious, moral, functional, and legal aspects. A rush to any kind of judgment obscures both their

106

identities and mutualities. The doctrinal resources of the Christian tradition point to their distinction but not separation. Further, this same doctrinal tradition — in both its commonalities and rich diversity — casts important light on Christian decision-making in every dimension of the present crisis. We ignore it at our peril.

PART II
Declaration Critics Respond

Not So Simple: Why I Didn't Sign

NICHOLAS WOLTERSTORFF

There's much in the "Declaration concerning Religion, Ethics, and the Crisis in the Clinton Presidency" that I find good and admirable, and with which I agree. Many of its signers are good friends of mine. Yet I find myself unable to sign on. Let me explain why. The Declaration has six points. With the last I have no difficulty. Concerning the other five, I think it is perhaps best for me to go down the points one by one, explaining what I find myself disagreeing with (referring to the points by number rather than quoting them).

Concerning 1

Let me begin by expressing my understanding of Clinton's appraisal of his own behavior vis-à-vis Monica Lewinsky. Assuming that Lewinsky's testimony on this point is correct, Clinton believes that what he was doing was morally wrong — believed it at the time, not just in retrospect. He is reported by her as saying, several times over, that what he was doing was wrong. This contrasts sharply with what we know of J. F. Kennedy's attitude toward his philandering: there's no indication that he ever thought it was wrong. Lest the comments that follow leave any doubt on the matter, I also believe that Clinton's behavior was morally wrong — and gross!

Clinton's self-recognition of doing wrong implies that, in this case,

111

we are not confronted with a person with low moral standards. We are confronted instead with a quite extraordinary case of weakness of will, at least when it comes to sexual temptation. Clinton's self-appraisal of his actions is a paradigmatic example of what St. Paul laments: "I do not understand my own actions. For I do not do what I want, but I do the very thing I hate" (Rom. 7:15-16).

Poll-takers over the past couple of years have taken to asking the public whether President Clinton shares their moral standards. Most reply that he does not. But I submit that one cannot determine a person's moral standards just from observing what he or she does. To suppose that one can ignores those troubling dynamics on which St. Paul put his finger: we find ourselves impelled to do what we know we ought not to do. Oh, who can deliver us!

My own conclusion from the discussion surrounding this case is that the President, the Congress, and the public alike have surprisingly high moral standards when it comes to sex — assuming that everybody is saying what they believe. I haven't heard anyone defend the President's activities, including the President himself. In its third point the Declaration observes that "by his own admission the President has departed from ethical standards."

At what point the President should have confessed his wrongdoing, and to whom, is not entirely clear to me. Whom one ought to tell about one's wrongdoing, and at what point one ought to do so, seems *often* to be unclear. But let me be as emphatic on one point here as I was on the other: the President's *deception* was morally wrong. Not voluntarily making his wrong actions public is one thing; deceiving is quite another. But rather than finding the President unusually corrupt on this point, as many seem to find him, I must say that I find him all too human — no different from most of us in his attempt to conceal what he knew was wrong and shameful. No different from King David, though in David's case something close to murder was also involved. I myself have never known of an extramarital affair in which the parties did not do their best to deceive people. Eventually, the President had no choice but to come clean.

What do you and I, as Christian believers, ask of someone who did what he knew to be wrong — particularly if that offender is a fellow Christian? We ask repentance of that person, and normally we ask for an *expression* of that repentance. As a component of the expression of repentance, we urge him to ask the forgiveness of those he wronged. If we ourselves are the wronged parties, it is then up to us whether to grant the forgiveness, assuming we judge the expression of repentance sincere.

As I understand it, this is exactly what President Clinton did at that famous (infamous) Religious Leaders' Prayer Breakfast. If he had failed to do this, failed to express repentance for his wrongdoing, and failed to ask forgiveness from those he had wronged, it would be right to chastise him for his failure. So I fail to understand why Clinton's expression of repentance, and his plea for forgiveness, have evoked such a hostile response in so much of the Christian community. What should he have done instead? The Declaration described what happened at the Prayer Breakfast as "a politically motivated and incomplete repentance," and cites the President's words as an example of "the political misuse of religion."

It's not clear to me what the Declaration regards as "incomplete" about Clinton's repentance. I can understand the person who regards the President's *expression* of repentance as *insincere;* one is faced with judging the sincerity of statements of repentance all the time. But I don't know what is meant by "incomplete" repentance. Further, as I have already noted, the Declaration itself says that "by his own admission the President has departed from ethical standards." As for myself, I don't see how Lewinsky's testimony as to what Clinton said when he was "engaging in sex" with her allows for any other interpretation than that he knew what he was doing was wrong when he was doing it.

Contrast what Clinton said with what Congressman Hyde said when his affair of some years back became known. Hyde described it as a "youthful indiscretion" (whether it was "youthful" when engaged in when he was in his forties is a nice question, but let that pass). In describing it as an "indiscretion," Hyde made no admission of *moral wrongdoing* whatsoever. It's extremely unusual for public figures to admit to *moral* wrongdoing. Nixon conceded only to having made mistakes. Clinton said that what he did was *morally wrong.*

Lewinsky's testimony unmistakably indicates, so far as I can see, that he believed what he said; without this testimony, those who claim that his expression of repentance was purely political would have had a fairly good case. But what about the fact that he tried to conceal what he had done? Well, the fact that a person doesn't want his actions to come to light hardly proves that he didn't consider them wrong, that he only wanted to keep them hidden for political reasons.

113

To say it once more: who of us, having done something shameful that we recognize to be wrong, would want it to come to light? My view, then, is that we should be gratified by Clinton's recognition that what he did was morally wrong, and should accept with gratitude his repentance and expression of repentance rather than reacting with sour grumpiness, as if he shouldn't have expressed repentance but should have said something else instead. Rejoice over the sinner who returns home.

Concerning 2

Conceding to Clinton no more than an "incomplete repentance," the Declaration suggests that his *expression* of repentance was designed to "avert serious consequences for wrongful acts." It then goes on to challenge "the widespread assumption that forgiveness relieves a person of further responsibility and serious consequences." I agree with the Declaration in rejecting this last assumption, though I think it's not all that widespread. But I myself am not aware of Clinton ever saying that he should receive no punishment for what he did; perhaps I have overlooked something. So far as I can tell, the issue for him has been the *level* of punishment. My understanding is that his lawyers have suggested censure of some sort rather than removal from office. So if there is that widespread assumption that the Declaration says there is, it strikes me that Clinton does not share it. He appears to me to distinguish the legal from the personal better than most.

Furthermore, the worry that the President might escape without punishment strikes me as very odd indeed. He has been placed in our model global equivalent of the stocks of an old New England town. The New Englanders regarded being put in the stocks as punishment. As I made clear above, I think we should be gratified by Clinton's recognition that what he did was not just "indiscreet" — as it certainly was — but morally wrong. Nonetheless, the Declaration is quite correct in saying that repentance normally does not remove the propriety of punishment, though often it has some bearing on the quality and severity of that punishment. On this point, however, the Declaration says that "the President continues to deny any liability for the sins he has confessed" (notice that the Declaration does acknowledge that he has "confessed sins"). But I don't know what "denying liability" means here.

He has confessed that he is *responsible* for having sinned, and he has acknowledged that it's *appropriate* for him to be punished.

Concerning 3

I firmly agree that "certain moral qualities are central to the survival of our political system." I'm dubious, however, that Clinton's behavior endangers that survival. He hasn't committed treason, bribed judges, violated explicit instructions of Congress, or anything of that sort. My own view is that the greatest current danger to the survival of our political system is the extreme partisanship which has invaded the system over the past fifteen years or so. At least at the national level, we no longer have, to any significant degree, a deliberative democracy in which our representatives debate what serves justice and the common good. We have little more than an *interest group* democracy. I do not think democracy can long survive if we, the citizens, and our representatives regard politics as simply a device for securing our own private interests. So I see the pervasiveness of interest group politics as currently the greatest moral threat to our political order.

I fail to see — perhaps I'm short of sight — that Clinton's behavior is going to unleash a flood of perjury, abuse of power, disrespect for the dignity of women, disregard for law, and so forth, thus endangering the endurance of our political system. So I disagree with the Declaration in its identification of what is today the principal moral threat to our civil order.

Concerning 4

As to "the impact of this crisis on our students": I cannot believe that, as the consequence of this fiasco, any student will be inclined to imitate Clinton's behavior, or to admire it. Everybody has condemned the behavior, including Clinton himself. So why would anybody be moved to imitate it? Granted, his behavior is likely to diminish the admiration that young persons have for their political leaders. But our political leaders haven't been all that admirable over the past fifteen years in any case. Perhaps it's the Calvinist in me that wants me to add that we had better not expect most of them to be admirable most of the time. One had

115

better not expect politicians to be one's moral leaders. Remember: the state is the polity of the human community in general, and human beings are "crooked timber."

Let me add an additional point, one I have already hinted at: President Clinton has been humiliated, by the combination of the Special Prosecutor's activities and those of the House Judiciary Committee, to a degree beyond the humiliation ever wreaked on any other President, and most other politicians. He has been publicly shamed across the world. For my part, I find such unbounded shaming to be a deeply troubling phenomenon. It would have shattered any one of us. I regret that the Declaration made no attempt to wrestle with the moral questions raised by this deliberate shaming. When New Englanders were put in stocks, only the village knew about it.

The Declaration goes on to speak of "the widespread desire to 'get this behind us,'" and judges this desire as not taking "seriously enough the nature of the transgressions and their social effects." A good many leaders and intellectuals have taken to chastising the American people for their response to the Lewinsky affair. The Declaration hereby joins this chorus, though in much more muted language than that used, for example, by William Bennett.

My own interpretation of the public's response is quite different from that presupposed by this dressing down of the American public for their low moral standards. I think the public feels that we have been watching our legal system go berserk. My own prediction is that Clinton's immoral sexual behavior will have no abiding effects whatsoever on our civil life — nor will his perjury, if perjury it proves to be. But the dynamics in our legal system that have led to this impasse will continue to trouble us for a long time.

Consider: a woman files a suit claiming that a good many years back she was propositioned by the President. The legal system then places him under oath and allows lawyers to ask him about any improper relations that he may have had with any woman whatsoever over, apparently, the span of his adult life. In the course of that deposition, he does his best to mislead the interrogators at some points. Perhaps he not only tries to mislead them; it may well be that he lies at some points, and it may well be that some of those lies constitute (legal) perjury. The system then allows a prosecutor to enter and do all he can to find out whether the President did or did not perjure himself; and beyond that, to present his findings in full, lurid, unexpurgated detail, without any of the witnesses having been cross-examined. (The reason I sound indecisive as to whether perjury was committed is that the original deposition, as well as the later one, consisted of lawyers trying to catch a lawyer. In that situation, as one would expect, a great deal of fine parsing of words occurs, along with the use of words designed to divert the attackers from their prey. It's difficult for us laypeople to penetrate the haze. And once again, lest one think President Clinton peculiarly culpable on this count, remember that Kenneth Starr similarly used language designed to mislead in his cross-examination by David Kendall on November 19. What helped us viewers spot Starr's evasions was that Kendall frequently caught him at it.)

The perjury laws are thus used to allow prosecutors and others to investigate activity that, apart from such laws, they would have to stay out of. Any activity that is itself entirely legal and not subject to the scrutiny of prosecutors and investigators is brought within their reach by getting the person into a situation where false answers to questions asked are criminal. If the activity is one that, though entirely legal, the person would, for whatever reason, prefer not to bring out in the public, he is faced with the distasteful choice of either bringing what is rightly private out into the public or perjuring himself. Either publicize the justifiably private or perjure yourself is the choice that the system succeeds in forcing on the defendant. And if there is any indication that he *might* have perjured himself, investigators may then investigate activity that they otherwise would have to stay out of. Our sexual harassment laws are proving extraordinarily useful for this purpose. Lacking direct evidence for the harassment claimed, prosecutors are allowed to introduce into evidence a pattern extending over as many years as they wish to investigate.

The Special Prosecutor repeats, like a mantra: "Perjury is inimical to our whole system of law." Of course it is. But to say only this is to turn a blind eye to the way in which the perjury laws, as they are now being used in conjunction with other laws, constitute a menace to our privacy. The argument offered against granting Secret Service officers immunity for testifying about the President is that they should be required to testify if they are witnesses to a crime on the part of the President. Of course they should. But they were not witnesses to a crime. They were witness to entirely legal behavior. It was, however, behavior that had been brought within the scrutiny of prosecutors by virtue of the President's having been forced to testify about the behavior in a situation where false answers would be criminal. No behavior whatsover on the part of the President — legal or illegal — is now, in principle, off limits to testimony by his Secret Service guards.

As I say, my impression of the response of the American people to this sorry episode in our history is that they discern what has been happening and regard our legal system as having gone berserk in its invasion of privacy. I share that view, and I regret that the Declaration chose to say nothing about the menace that this legal development represents. I am not consoled by the Special Prosecutor saying that everything he has done is legal, and that all he cares about is truth. Not everything that is legal to do is good to do; and there are some truths that the law had best not try to discover, lest the law become a menace to us all. To which I add this: an admirable feature of the American System up to this point has been its insistence that it is not only getting out the truth that counts but also how the truth is gotten out. Many cases have been thrown out of court because the truth was gotten in the wrong way. Truth is not the only issue in this case, or any other.

Concerning 5

I join the Declaration in urging our "society as a whole to take account of the ethical commitments necessary for a civil society." But as indicated above, I do not share its judgments concerning the location of imminent danger. The Declaration says that we "now confront a much deeper crisis" than partisan conflicts: "whether the moral basis of the constitutional system itself will be lost." I fail to see how this case threatens to undermine the moral basis of our constitutional system. My own guess is that our constitutional system will eventually do its work and censure the President for his behavior. Far from encouraging perjury, the disposition of the case will serve mightily to discourage it. The public will draw the conclusion that perjury gets punished — though rather often, of course, prosecutorial discretion means that it does not. What will remain after the censure has been issued and Clinton leaves the presidency is "partisan conflicts." Indeed, what is now happening in the House Judiciary Committee is a vivid example of what I abhor. The case before it is a sorry affair, but far more menacing for our future is the fact that the Committee is so filled with partisan rancor that it cannot deal responsibly with the case.

In summary, Clinton's sexual behavior was morally reprehensible. I, as a Christian, am gratified, however, that he himself apparently regards it as morally reprehensible; I am gratified that he has not dismissed it as an "indiscretion." It's his extraordinary weakness of will that I lament. I further condemn the systematic deception in which he engaged to try to keep the affair from coming to light. He should have "come clean," at least by the time of his deposition in the Paula Jones affair. But — and this may once again be the Calvinist in me coming to the surface — I do not regard such behavior as unusual. And as to threats to our future as a democracy, I do not regard the President's behavior as any great threat.

What threatens the future of our democracy is the specter of the legal system going berserk, as well as the interest group partisanship that not only predates this episode but has now thoroughly engulfed it.

A historian friend of mine tells me that one of the things that contributed to the collapse of the Roman Empire was that its political leaders ceased to discuss issues of justice and the common good, but instead began to conduct politics by harnessing the legal structure to the investigation of scandals and rumored scandals — politics by scandal-mongering and scandal investigation. I do not myself know whether he's right about that.

Why Truth Matters More than Justice

JOHN P. BURGESS

The "Declaration concerning Religion, Ethics, and the Crisis in the Clinton Presidency" is critically important to the current debate because it challenges us to examine the relationship of morality and politics more carefully. The Declaration rightly insists that the President's public display of repentance does not relieve him of responsibility for his actions. The Declaration appropriately questions the way in which moral language and moral actors, such as representatives of the church, have been (mis)used for political ends.

While developing an ethical analysis of the presidential crisis, the Declaration is also a political act. Some will read the Declaration as a courageous effort to hold accountable a President who has thus far escaped any penalty for his admitted misdeeds. Others, however, will dismiss it as just one more desperate effort to humiliate a President whose actions, while deplorable, do not warrant resignation or impeachment.

I share the Declaration's concern that the President be held accountable. But I believe that the Declaration misses a critical point: in politics, truth is sometimes more important than justice. Building on the Declaration, I wish to show more clearly how morality, law, and politics appropriately relate to each other, and why establishing the truth is sometimes the only kind of accountability possible in politics.

120

Levels of Ethical Analysis

To make sense of the presidential crisis, we need to look at several levels of ethical analysis. At one level, the questions are *moral*. By moral, I especially mean questions of personal integrity and interpersonal relationship, not questions of the President's relationship to the American people as a whole (which I label below as "political"). Did the President's actions violate moral standards of fidelity and truth telling? Did he betray the trust of particular individuals — his wife and daughter, his advisers, his cabinet? At a second level, the questions are *legal*. Did the President's actions violate the law? Are they criminal offenses? At a third level, the questions are *political*. Have the President's actions rendered him unable to serve effectively in office? Has he lost his ability to command respect and to lead the nation?

As facts have come to light — for the most part, by way of the Special Prosecutor's investigation, but also in the President's own admissions — each one of these levels of ethical analysis has been in play. Most people now agree that the President's actions constitute moral offenses, though the President and the public have struggled to find the right kind of moral language by which to characterize them. The President himself first admitted to an "inappropriate," indeed, a "wrong" relationship with Ms. Lewinsky, and to "misleading" people. Later, he agreed with Senator Lieberman's assertion that his actions had been "immoral." By the time of the Religious Leaders' Prayer Breakfast in Washington, the President had resorted to religious language of "sin."

How to evaluate the legal questions has been more difficult. To this day, the President and his lawyers have insisted that the President's answers under oath to Paula Jones's lawyers and to the grand jury were technically correct. In contrast, the President's critics have accused him either of perjury, a legal offense, or of "lying under oath," a less precise term that may or may not have legal consequences.

Questions at the political level have increasingly resolved themselves in favor of the President. Early concerns that the scandal would undermine his ability to lead the nation have diminished. Public opinion surveys have given the President consistently high ratings for his job performance, even though most Americans do not condone his admitted misdeeds. The mid-term elections further reinforced the public's confidence in the President's ability to govern.[1]

Resolving the Ethical Issues

Resolution of the presidential crisis involves resolution of issues at each of these levels of ethical analysis. At the moral level, the question is two-fold: what will restore the President's personal integrity, and what will restore the integrity of his interpersonal relationships.

Restoring personal integrity requires one to come to terms with the wrong that one has done to oneself. The question is not simply what one must do to regain others' trust, but what one must do to recover one's own moral core. Soon after his admission of wrongdoing, the President could have acted to restore his personal integrity by resigning. He chose, instead, to remain in office. But the question of personal integrity has not escaped him. He has asked three pastors to meet regularly with him and to keep him personally accountable. He has also recommitted himself to working harder than ever to execute the responsibilities of his office faithfully. (Thus he described his long hours in negotiating the Wye Accords as an act of "personal atonement.")

To skeptics, the President's refusal to resign simply signals his refusal to come to terms with his wrongdoing. But questions of personal integrity are not easily judged from afar. None of us can look into another's heart. We may never know whether the President has been able to develop a stronger moral core. He himself may never know. What is important is that he pose the question to himself, and that he examine himself.

Restoration of interpersonal relationship requires a person to come to terms with the wrong that one has done to others. One must seek to

---

1. A fourth level of ethical analysis, the *ecclesial* implications of the President's actions, has been almost entirely missing from the public debate. Church leaders have addressed the President primarily as a political leader, not as a member of an ecclesial community whose standards he violated. In another day and age, church leaders might have barred the President from the Lord's table until he had made confession, not simply to the nation but specifically to his brothers and sisters in Christ. Interestingly, several weeks after the Washington Prayer Breakfast, newspapers reported that the President had sent a letter to his congregation in Little Rock, asking for forgiveness.

restore trust where there has been betrayal. Different parties were injured by the President's actions in different ways. Different kinds of actions may now be required of the President, if relationship is to be restored. Some of the offended parties may be willing to forgive him simply on the basis of his public statements. Others, especially close family members and friends, may need to hear words of confession directly and privately from him. Still others may not be willing to grant him forgiveness until he has not just confessed his misdeeds but also made amends or suffered punishment.

Restoring relationship can be as difficult and elusive as restoring personal integrity. On the one hand, the President can ask for forgiveness, but he cannot demand it. He must listen and respond to those whom he has injured. On the other hand, those who have been injured cannot simply dictate the terms by which relationship will be restored. They must make an effort to understand why the President did what he did.

Resolution of the legal questions also poses difficult questions. What is the appropriate court of judgment? Is the President guilty of high crimes and misdemeanors that justify impeachment by the House and trial by the Senate? If not, should he be prosecuted in the courts? And when? Now, or after his term of office ends? The legal questions are further complicated by developments in the Jones case: the judge initially threw it out, and after the publicity about the President's relationship with Lewinsky, he settled out of court rather than risk having it reinstated. At this point, one might well ask, even if the President did commit perjury, should he now be prosecuted?

By contrast, the political question is largely resolved. Public opinion will not likely turn against the President. Yet, new developments on the moral and legal levels could have unexpected consequences. Were the First Lady publicly to state, for example, that she could no longer forgive the President, or were new evidence of perjury to be documented, public opinion could quickly change. The longer the case drags on, the greater its potential for affecting the President's ability to govern.

Interactions among These Levels of Ethical Analysis

The presidential scandal is further complicated by the ways in which these three levels of ethical analysis interact with each other. None exists in a vacuum. The President's public confessions — and his wife's and cabinet members' declarations of personal support — have operated not merely on a moral but also on a political level: they have shored up public support for the President. The legal questions, especially the nature of impeachment proceedings, have been affected by political realities: so long as the President's job-approval ratings have remained high, members of Congress have been less willing to move against him. If impeachment or criminal prosecution does proceed, moral and legal factors may eventually affect each other: in court cases, the defendant's moral demeanor may become a factor in how the court determines severity of punishment.

Yet, each level of analysis has its own integrity and should not be confused with the other two. In particular, the President's public confessions of wrongdoing have risked confusing moral and political categories. As the Declaration notes, the President — or at least some of the thinking in the public debate — has misused moral categories for the sake of political posturing. At times it has appeared that the President has been driven not by a firm, renewed, inner moral core but by public dissatisfaction with his initial address to the nation.

The confusion of moral and political categories has been compounded by the ability of modern communications to project the sense that each of us somehow has a personal relationship with the President. We have been tempted to believe that the President needed to confess to us, or that we needed to forgive him. Yet, as the Declaration notes, using moral categories in this way does "not function easily within the sphere of constitutional responsibility."

Ethical categories have become confused in other respects, as well. At times the Special Prosecutor has appeared overly zealous in applying legal categories to moral offenses. To many Americans, the possibility that the President committed perjury seems less clear — and less offensive — than the immorality of the President's relationship with Ms. Lewinsky and his efforts to hide it, and to discredit the Special Prosecutor's investigation. If the real problem in the President's actions has been sin, rather than crime, the law is not the proper vehicle for resolving the crisis, no matter how offensive his actions, and no matter how great the urge to hold him accountable.

Legal and political factors can also become confused. Political factors play an appropriate role in any criminal prosecution (the political climate often determines which crimes are prosecuted, and how vigorously), but the political cannot replace the legal. No one is above the law. While political factors are especially prominent in the case of impeachment, where the jury consists of elected representatives of the people, they do not absolve both House and Senate from making legal judgments. The President's popularity is not by itself sufficient reason to drop charges against him, if he is indeed guilty of criminal behavior.

The Needs of the Body Politic

The American public cannot tell the President how to restore personal integrity to his life, nor how to achieve reconciliation with those personal friends or family members who feel betrayed. Those whom the President has injured will have to wend their ways between the shoals of his ability to confess and their ability to forgive. They will be challenged to avoid both "cheap grace" and a desire for vengeance.

The American public cannot resolve intricate legal questions of what constitutes perjury or not. Such matters require the best thinking of the nation's legal minds. The American public does, however, deserve to know the truth about presidential behavior that has moral and legal consequences. The President is called to embody moral values and to uphold the laws of the land. While it is legitimate to guard against unwarranted intrusion into the President's private life, it is wrong to conclude that the public should know nothing of his moral and legal behavior. What the nation has needed has been not so much the President's apology or plea for forgiveness (as I have argued, these moral categories do not easily fit the political relationship that most of us have with the President), but his accounting of the truth. The President himself should have taken the initiative — from the outset, when first confronted about his relationship with Ms. Lewinsky, and later, when he had completed his testimony to the grand jury.

What needed to be documented was not intimate details of the President's relationship with Ms. Lewinsky but the President's lapses in judgment in having the affair, hiding it, then lying to and misleading the American people about it both through his own public statements and through those of his advisers.[2] Moreover, this truth telling needed to

2. It is notable — and troubling — that none of these advisors, as far as I know, has confessed his or her own complicity in promulgating these lies.

come not indirectly — by way of public airing of addresses to particular audiences (a church service, the Prayer Breakfast) — but directly, by way of a public address to the nation.

The strength of a democracy depends on citizens' ability to get at the truth about their leaders' conduct *of* office and *in* office, and then to make judgments about whether they are fit to serve. Tragically, the truth about Bill Clinton came to light only because of the efforts of the Special Prosecutor.[3] Yet we can be grateful that it did come to light, even if in more graphic detail than many Americans thought appropriate. Only the President and those whom he has personally offended can resolve the moral issues; only the Congress or the courts can resolve the legal issues; only the American public can resolve the political issues that arise, once the public knows the truth about his moral and legal behavior. In a parliamentary system, the way out of this crisis would have been to call an election. In our system, the next best thing has happened: public opinion polls and a mid-term election.

Why has the American public continued to support the President politically? It is instructive to examine the experience of democratizing nations as they have confronted the question of what to do with leaders of former, repressive regimes. In the heady experience of freedom, parts of the populace inevitably demand criminal prosecution of the old leaders. Others demand that the crimes of the past be forgotten — and the leaders of the old regime be granted amnesty — for the sake of preserving national unity. What the new regime often discovers is that documenting the truth of the crimes of the old regime is the best way to hold these two interests together. Justice is not entirely done, but neither are the crimes of the past entirely hidden. The public airing of the truth enables those who were oppressed by the old regime to know that they were in the right. Their voices become public and publicly legitimate.

The reluctance of the American public to bring President Clinton to justice surely reflects a sense of proportion: the immoralities of Bill Clinton pale in comparison to the crimes of the leaders of the old South Africa, Brazil, and the Soviet Union. But in another respect their reluctance parallels that of democratizing countries. The majority of Americans see Bill Clinton as best preserving the nation's political, economic,

3. While the President has contributed little to documenting the truth, his public statements have largely confirmed the facts that the Special Prosecutor has accumulated.

and social stability, despite his moral and possibly legal failings. They believe that his past wrongdoing has had no clear effect on the present and probably will not on the future. The public is largely satisfied that it knows the truth, and on the basis of what it knows, it is reluctant to support the President's resignation or impeachment.

When the Starr report became public, reporters conducted "man on the street" interviews all across the globe. Among those interviewed was a cab driver in Beijing, who exclaimed how wonderful America was: only in America, he said, could people find out the truth about the sexual escapades of their leaders without fear of being persecuted for knowing the truth and speaking it publicly.

Has Bill Clinton escaped justice? Is he the comeback kid who can avoid all responsibility for his actions? We should be disturbed that powerful people sometimes escape consequences that lesser people cannot. But in politics, truth may be more important than justice and is by itself no mean achievement. Not even a congressional censure would truly hold the President accountable. But it would further confirm what does matter: the truth.

On the Other Hand

LEWIS SMEDES

I really wanted to sign the scholars' Declaration — until I read it a second time. I share their belief that integrity is the core of good leadership, and I share their indignation about President Clinton's wretched lies. But I had enough misgivings about their arguments and their conclusions to persuade me that I could be more useful by explaining my doubts about their Declaration than by signing it.

Had someone asked me six years ago, would you want the sort of man who is capable of engaging in sexual relations — in the Oval Office at that — with an employee young enough to be his daughter, and then lied about it, over and over again, would you want that sort of man to be your President? My answer would be, "No, that is not the sort of man I would want to be our President." Well it turns out that our President is this sort of man. So now what?

The scholars believe that, being this sort of man, the kind we would not choose to be President, he should resign or, since he has not resigned, Congress should impeach him. And they offer some substantial reasons why they think so. It seems to me that the most important of them are these three:

1. His repentance is insincere, or worse, cynical.
2. He is accountable even if he is forgiven.
3. He lacks the moral character we need in our leader.[1]

---

1. I will in my response not be discussing the question of whether Mr.

128

I want to poke around a bit into the scholars' reasons why Mr. Clinton, unworthy as he is, should resign or be impeached. First, then, about the sincerity of Clinton's remorse:

We all know that the President confessed his sins and expressed his sorrow to a group of pastors in September. But the scholars think he was not sincere. They believe that he donned sackcloth as a political gimmick. He was not confessing before God; he was exploiting the men and women of God. What makes the scholars think so? Any truly remorseful President would have backed up his confession of sin with the one work that would have been "meet for" his repentance — his resignation. In failing to do the one thing necessary, he exposed his insincerity.

Wait a minute. The pastors who heard his confession did not think they were being exploited. Being right there in the room with him, they might have had a better sense of what was really going on in Bill Clinton's soul than the rest of us who were looking at snippets of his confession on the tube. Can we not assume that the ministers who were right there and heard the whole thing have as clear an eye for a presidential con job as scholars have from long distance?

Let's grant that the President's repentance was not perfectly pure. Should this surprise us? Must it invalidate his remorse? I do not think that I have ever confessed my sins without sneaking in a tincture of the self-serving. ("Look at what a splendid penitent I am, O Lord.") I dare say that in the entire history of penitential sobbing no sinner has ever shed a ninety-nine and nine-tenths percent pure tear. Our souls are too shifty for uncorrupted remorse. Why then should the scholars demand unalloyed remorse from the President?

But if he were sincere when he groveled, would he not have resigned then and there. What about the "works meet for repentance"? And what work could have been more "meet" at that moment than the work of resignation? Maybe. But, though it may be hard for some of us to swallow, it is also possible that the President sincerely believed that resigning with a swarm of crises swirling around the world would have done the nation more harm than good? And must we not at least grant that he might have chosen to leave his political fate up to Congress rather than taking it on himself to decide? We may doubt his judgment, but must we *assume* his insincerity?

Clinton's wrongdoings constitute an impeachable offense. My response is only to the question of Mr. Clinton's moral character.

But the scholars spy yet another instance of insincerity. Asking those three eminent pastors to be his spiritual directors, what could this have been but one more political ploy? How so? It was the publicity he gave it. For the scholars, the fact that it made the evening news tells us that he was once again using unwary men and women of God for his own questionable ends.

I just cannot see it their way. It seemed perfectly natural to me that Mr. Clinton should reassure the country that their flawed and failed President is seeking spiritual counsel. I know that I was glad to hear about it. Especially since the ministers he invited are known as much for their spiritual toughness as for their spiritual discernment.

We all know, I suppose, that crafty presidents have exploited innocent clergy for whatever political profit they could spin out of it. Billy Graham could tell Clinton's three counselors a thing or two about the risk of being used by men of power. But the fact that some preachers *can* be used does not mean that these preachers *are* being used. It is possible to be *useful to* even this President without being *used by* him. I trust these uncommonly savvy ministers to be well-tuned to the risk they are taking, and I am thankful they are willing to take it.

All in all, the scholars' suspicions seem more cynical than scholars need to be. Which brings us to the second reason the scholars think the President should go: being forgiven does not remove the President's accountability for what he has done.

Right. It seems to me that most people would agree that even if he is forgiven, the President should take the consequences of what he was forgiven for. The Pope may have forgiven the man who shot him, but the gunman had to do his time. And a President may be forgiven and still have to take the rap.

So why don't I give the scholars this and skip it? It's because I want to make still another observation about forgiving presidents. In the sort of national morass the President has pulled us into, national forgiveness is quite a murky matter. Common sense tells us that the only person qualified to forgive any sinner — even presidential sinners — is the person who was sinned against, the one who felt the wound, the victim. Who were the President's victims? Certainly his family, his friends, his cabinet members, and other political associates to whom he lied. And they may be having a devil of a time with God's way of dealing with having been sinned against. But how far does the circle of offense stretch?

God has a right to forgive us for the injuries we do to the least of his children, because when we injure them we injure their Father. I know that if you injure my children you also injure me. And so I have the right to forgive you even if you lay no finger on me. But do I have the right to forgive the Hutus for wronging the Tutsis? Palestinians for injuring Jews? White masters for making slaves of black people? My right to forgive them, it seems to me, depends much on whether my own soul is closely enough bound to the victims to be and to feel as victimized as they are.

Who, on this basis, has the right to forgive the President? Only those who actually *feel* the sting of having been wronged by him. I do not concede the right to forgive to people who lick their chops at Clinton's fall from grace and spitefully wait for his fall from office. Let only those who were there and who personally felt deeply injured and wronged by Bill Clinton even think about forgiving him.

Which brings us now to the third and clearly the most important of the scholars' concerns: the President's character. Leadership, they say, is "inherently about morality." I say amen to that. A bad person is more likely to be a bad leader than a good person is. When we talk about being bad or good persons, we are, of course, talking about character — about the moral sorts of persons we are. We betray the sorts of persons we *are* by the sorts of things we *do*. But a person who does one bad thing — or, as St. Paul put it, is "overtaken in a fault" — is not by that token a bad person. He is certainly a flawed person, but not necessarily an out-and-out bad person. It also depends on how bad the bad thing is. You need to do bad things, really bad things, and do them regularly and predictably, to qualify as a really bad person. Has President Clinton persistently and predictably done mostly bad things? He is flawed, of course, but is he bad enough to disqualify him from being the nation's leader? He is certainly not a saint, but is he a scoundrel?

How good a person must a President be? We cannot expect a politician to be a saint. (A saint would not apply for the job and would not get it if she did, and if she did get it, she probably would not be good at it.) But we can at least expect her to be something better than a scoundrel. So we have to put up with something in between. We settle for a president — as we do with friends and neighbors — who is both saint and scoundrel, imperfect in every way, corrupt in some ways and pretty good in others, good and bad mixed together and shaken down into the complex being each of us is. Maybe there is a laser line somewhere that cleanly separates tolerable imperfection from intolerable corruption. But who knows where it is drawn? We know it only when we see it, and not all of us have enough character to see it when it breathes in our faces.

America has done amazingly and embarrassingly well with its imperfect presidents. Especially with those whose fault line crossed through their hormones. The father of our country carried on a long love affair with the wife of a friend. Thomas Jefferson fathered at least one child with a beautiful slave girl and kept her as his mistress while owning her as a slave, and then disowned the child they conceived together. Franklin Roosevelt kept an affair with another woman going while his wife was out tirelessly fighting for his causes. Then we have the spectacular shenanigans of Camelot. And these are only the *sexual,* not the worst of all sins!

When it comes to serious character failures that could disqualify a presidency, I invite a comparison void of the sexual factor. Take Theodore Roosevelt's obscenely obsessive love of war, any war, and with anybody who got in our way, as long as it was a bloody bully war and as long as our side won. Surely he had a character defect most unwanted in a national leader. Yet Teddy Roosevelt was better at being President than many others who have held the job since. Compare him with the two Adamses, John and his son John Quincy. In them you had men of outspoken and insufferable moral righteousness, incorruptible, as famously flawless as the Hope diamond. Yet, neither of them rates more than a passing grade as a leader of the country. Single termers at that. My point is that one flaw does not make one a bad President and that total rectitude does not make one a good President.

The difference between Clinton's sins and the sins of Presidents past seems to be not that his are qualitatively worse but that we all know about his, and the public did not know about the sins of the others. The shameful private sins of other Presidents stayed private, and what the people did not know did not seem to hurt them much. What makes Clinton's sins less tolerable than the sins of his presidential fathers is not that his are intrinsically more shameful than theirs but that we are *all* shamed by them. And we are shamed by them because we all know all about them.

"No, no," the scholars (and other discerning readers) will protest. What makes sexual morality important to leaders is that character flaws tend to be organically tied to the rest of our characters, so that immoral-

132

ity in one thing leads to immorality in other things. Maybe, but I don't believe it is necessarily true. In what crucial national crisis did Bill Clinton betray us? In his masterful efforts to bring peace to the Middle East? In his peacemaking in Ireland? In his response to the horrors in the former Yugoslavia? In his deliberate way of coping with a mad Saddam? In his working out a balanced budget with the Republicans? And if not in these almost life-and-death (political) matters, then where?

No, it goes back to that one difference: *we all know about this President's sins.* We not only know that the President sinned, we know every shaming detail about his sins. And how do we know so much? We know it because a shameless media, an obsessed prosecutor, and a vindictive Congress determined that we should know. Clinton, like other and even greater Presidents, has sinned, but he alone, unlike the others, shames us. He shames us because we know too much. Clinton gave them the bullet, and they used it to fill us full of shame.

The scholars deplore the fact that many Americans are so content with the present economy that they close their eyes to the President's bad behavior. I would ask them to consider this: Maybe, for many people, a good economy means the difference between having a job and not having a job, and having a job is the difference between having and not having enough money to feed their children. And, to be honest about it, I feel a twitch when snugly tenured and amply pensioned scholars bitch about working people who put having jobs a notch above the presidential sexual sins in their value scale. Besides, how do the scholars know that people who don't want the President to fall are thinking only of money in their pockets? Maybe they are thinking of peace and justice as well.

People who want the President to stay drive William Bennett to ask: Where is the outrage? I can tell him where mine is. I am outraged at the way Bennett's friends in Congress predictably bow their knees to the National Rifle Association whenever guns are an issue. I am outraged that no President since Lyndon Johnson has had the courage to keep before our conscience the black smog of poverty that chokes all hope out of the people who live in our inner cities. I am fiercely angered, shamed, and deeply disappointed by Bill Clinton — but not quite outraged. Outrage I leave to the saints, the scholars, and the Christian Coalition.

133

Sex, Lies and Tapes:
The Case of Bill Clinton
and Catholic Teaching

WILLIAM J. BUCKLEY

For many contributors to this volume, the key crisis in the Clinton presidency is that his travails might not lead to a constitutional crisis and do not signal an electoral crisis. Indeed, there are voices in the Catholic tradition that could regard this state of affairs as yet another sign of widespread cultural relativism (*Veritatis Splendor, Evangelium Vitae;* Kavanaugh in *America,* October 17, 1998). They are probably right. On the other hand, there are other usually prolific Catholic voices whose silence has been deafening. Still others have incisive remarks about shame and presidential sexual dysfunction that might strike one as diagnostically apt, if not exculpatory (Callahan in *Commonweal,* November 6, 1998). They could also be correct. Of course, those sympathetic with the first group of Catholics might see any claims about diminished accountability as accommodationist to the kind of therapeutic hermeneutic that pervades so much political, religious, and moral language about the whole matter. This, too, might be true.

However, there are others who aim to retrieve how Catholic traditions can bring considerations of justice and equity to bear on moral assessment of the kind of presidential public carnival that many unfairly associate only with Jerry Springer's televised cockfights among the tragically undereducated. Charges about marital infidelity and dishonesty have long histories not confined to one class.

This essay has four parts: (1) after a brief narrative (figuration) of what has happened, I offer an initial legal and moral redescription (configuration) of these events on the basis of a traditional act-centered and virtue-based morality in Catholic ethics as laid out chiefly in the new universal *Catechism of the Catholic Church*. I follow these remarks with (2) a series of twelve qualifications (reconfigurations) from Catholic tradition (once again drawing upon the Catechism) and then (3) several observations about how a mistaken assumption that "consenting sex is private" undergirds erroneous appraisals of what is at stake in the discussion. Following these hermeneutic regressions, I conclude the essay (4) by reframing some of the moral issues at stake — especially how the unwillingness to talk about issues of sexuality robs us of the chance to reflect on how issues of gender and justice are involved.

In Catholic tradition, repentance and forgiveness have a communal context that aims to balance the needs of individuals and communities by acknowledging limits to the obligation to truth telling and reminding us of the exigencies of just reparation. Recurrent criteria from Catholic tradition mentioned in truth telling are instructive: balance justice and charity. As in discussions by Christians generally, positions can be caricatured: those insisting on charitable interpretations of Clinton's remorse can be dismissed as gullible; those who focus on justice as retributive — and further equate it with punishment — might harbor suspicions about Clinton's repentance that appear to others to cast doubt on the mercy of God. But we do not have to caricature, to be gullible, or to be overly restrictive in our interpretation of justice.

Even if his sexual escapades don't seem as serious as at least one of his namesakes, William Jefferson Clinton's woes place him in the undistinguished category of other recent Presidents. Yet dishonesty and obstruction of justice are different matters. It is one measure of the adversarial structure of our legal system (whose goals are less to seek truth than to adjudicate interests) and its susceptibility to the highly partisan posture of our legislative system that many find consolation in the fact that there are well-recognized legal limits to our obligations to help our legal "opponents." As any can tell you who have been involved in legal domestic work, issues of intimacy are better mediated than litigated; however, charges of obstructing justice and witness tampering surely deserve public scrutiny.

I

For a narrative overview (or figuration) of the facts and their contending interpretations, see *The Starr Evidence,* edited by Phil Kuntz (New York: Pocket Books/Simon and Schuster, 1998). So many facts leave us with an important question: What is to be the appropriate unit of moral analysis: the relationship, intimacies, efforts to conceal it, the Prayer Breakfast?

Likewise, interpretive traditions *configure* or structure these facts in different ways. Legally, the issue can be precisely stated: because consensual (although adulterous) intimacy is not normally grounds for impeachment, political focus turns to charges of perjury and obstruction of justice. Morally and religiously, was the Prayer Breakfast a disingenuously ritualistic display of politically expedient remorse designed to escape public if not legal accountability? Or, based on the testimony of those who have confidential knowledge about the President's sincerity, were these confessional statements made deeply and from the heart as the President's pastor Philip Wogaman has asserted? Were Lewinsky's alleged sexual intimacies a youthful romance gone awry or the unbridled fantasies of an ambitious and sexually experienced conniver? Was this a midlife crisis or yet one more chapter in the disturbing story of Clinton's predatory and consumerist objectifications of women? Do "sexual indiscretions" (what Clinton called "inappropriate intimacies") in the context of (what might be) a troubled marital relationship constitute "marital infidelity"? Were efforts to conceal such behaviors inappropriate or objectionable? There is plenty of future work for those wishing to intersect the full *Starr Report* with some of the "masters of suspicion" of sexuality in our own era — whether Freud, Foucault, MacKinnon, or Posner.

Let us concisely *configure* some of the issues at stake in the charges of sexual impropriety and dishonesty (which includes obstruction of justice) from the vantage point of one traditional Catholic account of an act- and virtue-centered morality, as attested by the universal *Catechism of the Catholic Church* (CCC). The task is not made easy because (1) the CCC combines elements of an ethic of action, duty, and virtue (2) which are then variously justified, sometimes on a natural law basis grounded in a theology of creation (with an accompanying ontology of goodness, e.g., #1718, 1803, 1810, 1954), at other times on a more complicated theology of the covenant, with appeals to the Trinity (combining creation, sanctification and redemption: 1692ff., 1997, 1720-21). For historical and institutional reasons, claims about right and wrong actions have their pedigree in assessments that confessors were called to make as to whether or not a given behavior was sinful. Hence moral language about right and wrong actions in the Catechism tends to be objectivist, definitional, and distinction-oriented as well as retrospective. On the other hand, the language of goods and bads (virtues and vices) finds its home in traditions of spiritual formation, advice giving and direction, which, until recently, were largely the domain of religious communities, clergy, and their secular counterparts in therapy and counseling. As reflected in the CCC, this language tends to be exhortative for the subject being spiritually counseled, visionary about worthy ideals and prospectives.

Were one to focus on discrete negative acts, or vices that oppose the sixth and ninth commandments, there are three categories of acts relevant in this case: lust, masturbation, and infidelity/adultery. Although the relevant sections of the Catechism share a Decalogue framework, the Catechism generally aims to start not with pathologies but with the goods and virtues that wrong actions oppose. As a "disordered desire for or inordinate enjoyment of sexual pleasure," lust (CCC #2351) opposes the virtue of chastity, which is a kind of subvirtue of the natural virtue of temperance that is completed by the theological virtue of charity (self-mastery is a part of the formation for self-donation, 2346). The virtue of chastity aims for an integration of sexuality within the person (bodily and spiritually) that includes an apprenticeship in self-mastery that is a long and exacting training in human freedom requiring personal effort, cultural support, and God's grace (2337-2345). Alleged phone sex or masturbation opposes the virtue of chastity by disordering the gift of self to another, which should blossom in friendship (2346-7, 2352); in highly coded language, it has been termed "intrinsically and gravely disordered action" that frustrates "the total meaning of mutual self-giving." In contrast to moral appraisals about what offends the virtue of chastity, adultery/ infidelity offends the dignity of marriage and is an injustice that injures the sign of the covenant, the rights of the other spouse, the institution of marriage, the good of human generation, and the welfare of children (2380-2381). These categories echo the ancient categories of the goods of marriage from Augustine of *proles* (procreation), *fides* (mutual service including exclusivity and monogamy), and *sacramentum* (the symbolic stability of permanence and indissolubility) but also, and especially more recently, elaborated goods such as spousal love and marital friendship (*Humanae Vitae, Familiaris Consortio, Donum Vitae,* etc.).

The eighth commandment defines false witness, perjury, and lying as wrong actions that are in opposition to the virtue of truthfulness. These offenses constitute a refusal to commit oneself to moral uprightness and are "fundamental infidelities to God," which are said to undermine the foundations of the covenant (2464). Later in the text, the "contrary to nature" argument is used (2485; "the purpose of speech is to communicate known truth to others"). Because it is pertinent to discussions below, the text merits lengthy direct quotation:

(2477) False witness and perjury. When it is made publicly, a statement contrary to the truth takes on a particular gravity. In court it becomes false witness (Prov. 19:9). When it is under oath, it is perjury. Acts such as these contribute to condemnation of the innocent, exoneration of the guilty, or the increased punishment of the accused (Prov. 18:5). They gravely compromise the exercise of justice and the fairness of judicial decisions.

(2478) Respect for the reputation of persons forbids every attitude and word likely to cause them unjust injury (Code of Canon Law, 220). He becomes guilty:

- of *rash judgment* who, even tacitly, assumes as true, without sufficient foundation, the moral fault of a neighbor;
- of *detraction* who, without objectively valid reason, discloses another's faults and failings to persons who did not know them (Sir. 21:28);
- of *calumny* who, by remarks contrary to the truth, harms the reputation of others and gives occasion for false judgments concerning them.

After noting that "every word or attitude is forbidden which by flattery, adulation or complaisance encourages and confirms another in malicious acts and perverse conduct" (2480), a crucial definition of lying is given from Augustine: "A lie consists in speaking a falsehood with the intention of deceiving" (2842).

In short, to the extent that Clinton (or Lewinsky) lusted, masturbated, was adulterous, lied or perjured himself, such wrong actions offended virtues that aim for goods that are worthy of human dignity and generally conducive to human flourishing (both personal and social). If done voluntarily and with knowledge, such actions are wrong and in religious terms sinful — even though, according to Catholic teaching, no one can judge definitively the state of grace of another living person (e.g., 2005). Were someone to object that none of the parties is Catholic, Catholic tradition would reply that these moral categories are not exclusively Catholic. In accord with Christian traditions echoed from Augustine, Aquinas, Luther, and Calvin about the limits of the civil law regarding immoral behavior, it should be noted that such immoralities as occurred do not by themselves constitute an endorsement of some specific legal response. A separate argument must still be made about the legal suitability of any number of responses.

II

We now *reconfigure* these initial evaluative conclusions by returning to the CCC to see what qualifications are offered and why. As we shall see, Catholic tradition is not content to merely state what is right, condemn what is wrong, exhort to what is good, or caution against what is bad. Catholic tradition looks to its own history with suspicion and retrieval to offer a political economy of reconciliation and forgiveness. Although these criteria could be used to criticize both Clinton and Starr, perhaps instead they can help our national conversation.

1. The first qualifications concern *sexual improprieties*. Most of us hardly need to be reminded of the CCC's claim that the self-mastery involved in chastity is "long and exacting work" (2342). Philip Wogaman follows a long tradition in appraising Clinton's "sins of the flesh" (weakness) less seriously than malice. This difference rests on a distinction between moral and intellectual virtues (but ignores some troubling admissions Clinton is alleged to have made to Lewinsky about how and why he made a decision to get involved with her). However, at least three problems emerge. The rational bifurcation between intellect and will that stands behind this schema has been criticized by Thomists (and non-Thomists) as a kind of scholastic architectonic that neglects the dynamic and fluid account of Aquinas on the passions, reasons, and dispositions (e.g., compare Gilby, Finnis, de Sousa). There is a unity to character that one should not dichotomize. Secondly, writers on virtue could well express concern that passions and dispositions cannot defensibly be said to

139

be under the control of some transhistorical account of reason or intellect available from one particular tradition (MacIntyre, *Which Justice, Which Rationality?*). Third, the CCC is clear that chastity is not just reducible to self-control but involves others. As I see it, Catholic tradition at its best testifies to a Gospel that constantly confronts rhetorics of human flourishing. It is here that I think some of what the Catholic tradition has to say about sexuality and gender justice (discussed below) is so counter-cultural and necessary for this conversation.

2. Rather than attempt to resolve the "justice" versus "charity" interpretations of the Prayer Breakfast, remaining qualifications illustrate how considerations of justice *and* charity should enter into the conversation *about Clinton's alleged perjury.* Following Aquinas, the CCC construes truthfulness in relation to the mutual confidence necessary for civil society (2469). Hence, the virtue of truth is decisively related to justice, or "giving another his due." However, drawing truthfulness into Aristotle's doctrine of virtue as the mean between two extremes has implications that paradoxically *limit what should be said* and what should be known. "Truthfulness keeps to the just mean between what ought to be expressed and what ought to be kept secret: it entails *honesty and discretion.*" Although "[t]ruth or truthfulness is the virtue which consists in showing oneself true in deeds and truthful in words, and guarding against duplicity, dissimulation, and hypocrisy," candor is not equated with explicitness or complete disclosure. Regrettably, no examples are offered about how to balance honesty and discretion.

3. As quoted extensively above, "false witness under oath is perjury" (2476), but respect for persons forbids "unjust injury" and detraction or "disclosing another's fault's and failings to persons who did not know them . . . without objectively valid reason" (2477). Harming the reputation of others is also proscribed. Note that prior to the establishing of the truth of charges alleged, the balance between the right to know and the rights of the individual are tilted in the accused individual's presumed right to a reputation.

4. Citing Ignatius of Loyola's *Spiritual Exercises,* the CCC states: "To avoid rash judgments, everyone should be careful to *interpret insofar as possible his neighbor's thoughts, words, and deeds in a favorable way*" (2478). Although the champion of discernment in the spiritual life will hardly endorse being gullible, it seems reasonable to ask whether Clinton's advisors have been overly indulgent in confronting his behavior.

140

5. Augustine's ostensibly simple definition of lying as "speaking a falsehood with the intention of deceiving" (2482) contains deceptive subtleties. The falsehood must be known to be such (otherwise it is ignorance) and deliberately deceptive. Exactly who must know this and how are open to debate. Even though courts have experience adjudicating the evidentiary requirements for assessing one's knowledge and intentions, their judgments are not a guarantee of truthfulness — even though they are probative. When courts act impartially, they invite our trust; however, when a process of truth finding cannot evoke trust because of suspicions about its partisan agenda, and when the person being questioned admits misrepresenting himself to "game" this system and mislead the public, it is hard to know how simple definitions or appeals to the virtue of truth telling can remedy all that ails the process, much less scrutinize any lies. Starr was right to chide Clinton if he lied simply because he did not like the questions or questioners; however, Starr may have missed a point central to Catholic tradition: disclosure of the truth is relevant to social context. At this point, terminological subtleties also begin to matter.

6. The next section introduces nuances and subtleties that have long been the object of scorn and reproach. "To lie is to speak or act against the truth in order to lead into error someone who has the right to know the truth" (2483). This sentence bristles with stipulative terms and phrases loaded with historical experiences and conceptual distinctions: "to speak or act against the truth" (instead of "falsehood") and "in order to lead into error" (instead of "with the intention of deceiving"), as well as this commandment's first discussion about "the right to know the truth." The notion of the "right to know the truth" grew out of terrible persecutions, unjust regimes, and coercive efforts to induce self-incriminating claims. Later some would expand the hedges on truth telling to escape onerous responsibilities, and a notion of a "mental reservation" became pejoratively synonymous with "equivocation" (as well as "hair-splitting," "casuistry," and "Jesuitical") in ways famously pilloried by Pascal's *Pensées*. Speaking "against the truth in order to lead into error" connotes more than a passive toleration for misunderstanding but a colluding in misinterpretation, as well as a logical distinction between what contradicts the truth and what is contrary to it. In short, for good historical reasons and important conceptual distinctions, the injunction to simple "truth telling" is actually quite complex. The fact that such valid distinctions can be abused does not ne-

gate what important nuances they remain. They reveal what Catholic tradition has discovered, sometimes quite painfully, in its own history: we do not need a perfect society before we should be honest — but heedless candor can lead to needless injustice. The jury is still out as to whether Clinton's admitted misleadings of family, staff, and public include perjury during a trial.

7. The *seriousness* of a lie varies according to numerous criteria: "the nature of the truth it deforms, the circumstances, the intentions of the one who lies, and the harm suffered by its victims"; the kind of injury done to the virtues of justice and charity (2484). These stipulations permit honest disagreements about what a lie has done, as well as empirical claims and counterclaims that try to minimize or maximize the results of a lie.

8. Because lying is a violence done to another, which is also destructive to society by undermining trust among "men" (2486), it entails a *limited duty of reparation,* "even if its author has been forgiven" (2487). "When it is impossible publicly to make reparation for a wrong, it must be done secretly" (2487). Although this discussion perhaps reflects an "interpersonal" bias, some could find in it the seeds for Clinton's refusal to admit personal wrongdoing at the Prayer Breakfast — which could lead to charges of a felony. Once again, the notion of what is "impossible" for the President to admit is highly contentious.

9. While lying is not endorsed, there is *limited permission for refusing to being entirely forthcoming.* "The right to the communication of the truth is not unconditional. . . . This requires us in concrete situations to judge whether or not it is appropriate to reveal the truth to someone who asks for it" (2488). The criteria for appropriateness include "charity and respect for the truth, the good and safety of others, respect for privacy, and the common good . . . are sufficient reasons for being silent about what ought not be known or for making use of a discreet language. The duty to avoid scandal often commands strict discretion" (2489). Of course, questions abound as to who should judge such criteria — or as to whether or not they are so widely stated as to permit anyone to refuse to admit to anything incriminating. Furthermore, note how false understandings of the criteria could lead to unwanted results: for example, a cultural bias that "consenting sexual encounters" are private is contrary to much in Catholic tradition about the communitarian (social, not just interpersonal) nature of sexuality. Nonetheless, note how the criteria are those of both justice and charity. Even though

legally permissible (because some of the questions were vague), was Clinton's aforementioned "gaming the system" by not being forthright an example of his judgments about "appropriateness" ("I don't have to help them . . .")?

10. With respect to *professional secrets,* "Even if not confided under the seal of secrecy, private information prejudicial to another is not to be divulged without a grave and proportionate reason" (2491). Once again, unfortunately, general criteria are offered without examples (serious to whom? proportionate to what and according to whom?).

11. "Everyone should observe an appropriate reserve concerning persons' private lives" (2492). In a quote pertinent to any who leaked information, as well as to the news media: "Those in charge of communications should maintain a fair balance between the requirements of the common good and respect for individual rights. Interference by the media in the private lives of persons engaged in political or public activity is to be condemned to the extent that it infringes upon their privacy and freedom" (2492).

12. Although the CCC does not do so, the duty to make reparation for a lie could well extend to a duty for reparation for refusing to disclose the whole truth (2487). Once again, considerations of justice and charity are crucial.

In sum, these *reconfigured* qualifications from Catholic tradition aim to reframe the issues in a larger and more nuanced justice-charity framework. By eschewing simplifications, this enlargement invites the criticism that a normative (much less prophetic) edge to a religious tradition has now evaporated in a kind of sulk to social conventions that presumably should be kept stable. As noted below, this is anything but our intention.

III

To rebut the charge that we are urging a do-nothing approach that exculpates Clinton (or Starr), we must get at a key issue behind lying, the Prayer Breakfast, and many commentaries. It is not difficult to be dismissive of Clinton's biblical *sexegesis* (oral sex is nowhere condemned in the Bible) — as well as his own "casuistry" concerning what he does and does not consider morally problematic nonspousal *sexperience* (sexual intimacy without intercourse). Nor is it difficult from Catholic tradition to criticize definitions he uses by appealing to what most Americans think ("sexual relationship" includes sexual intercourse but excludes oral sex). Even as the magisterial Church and theologians recalibrate understandings and priorities among the personal, interpersonal, and social goods of marriage, a critical personalism in Catholic ethics can be a powerful antidote to the powerfully commodified privatizations of eros (and family) in fin de siècle North American culture as exemplified in Clinton's case (Hauerwas, Anderson et al., Giddens, Kavanaugh).

Sex is not private, but it is certainly personal in Catholic teaching. Of course, personalism has many faces, sexual consumerism has many manifestations, and the sexual revolution has had many victims: although contraceptives are widely available and used, half of all births occur to single women; a third to half of all pregnancies end in abortion; we have doubled our life span, yet serial monogamy is a reality facing half of all marriages; we live and work with blended families, domestic partnerships, and one in four women is sexually abused, typically by a spouse or significant other. Ours is a culture that needs a renewed and retrieved Catholic tradition of sexuality that is beyond oppressive conjugalizations but truly liberating for men and women (Cahill, Jung, Patrick). The widespread belief that sex is a private affair of personal consumption distorts a great deal of the truth about its connectedness to wider natural processes and social relationships. Catholic tradition offers a more ecological understanding of sexuality.

Consider briefly how countercultural this is to widely shared appraisals of Clinton's mistakes: Whether in the "economy" of salvation or the "marketplace" of ideas, few will "buy" the idea that adulterous but consensual sex will "cost" a person eternal life even if they must somehow be "accountable." Why? Whether or not sex is any "big deal," such behavior is presumptively a "private account" that should not be "charged" against a person, although one should "settle" with family and "compensate" victims at whose "expense" one has "indulged oneself." Whether or not this is "cheap grace," the "cost of discipleship" should not be at the "expense of family life," "risk to reputation," or the "price of the presidency." Clinton should be able to "bargain" with his accusers.

Thus the ethos of late consumer capitalism has so shaped some of the central linguistic categories and moral assumptions of our age that reflection about Clinton's situation is reducible to the transactional metaphors of one kind of commutative justice. Small wonder that religious and moral language about this issue is so "marginalized."

IV

Finally, let me briefly offer a few conclusions:

1. Disturbing questions about the complicity of Monica Lewinsky cannot disguise the powerful forces of prosecutorial and presidential prowess, prerogatives, and patriarchy exercised on many women to try to cover and uncover this whole affair. Asymmetrical power relations among a President, an intern/employee, secretary, first lady, and others have led to many being pressured into keeping up appearances. A gender justice of relationships and trust calls for greater scrutiny of intimacy in asymmetrical role relations. Even though Clinton's sexual intimacies with Lewinsky would bore student audiences of "Straight Talk about Sex" on TV or at most dorms in Catholic Colleges, there was clearly an abuse of a fiduciary relationship.

2. In addition to questions about the just use of resources, even Ken Starr could not survive a forty-million-dollar investigation of his past. From the Middle Ages through the early modern period, both Catholics and Protestants upheld as a fundamental principle that "no one is compelled to reveal his own secret sin" *(nemo tenetur detegere turpitudinem suam)* or can be compelled to reveal "private and shameful acts." In fact, to try to do so will merely "give occasion of horrid perjuries. . . ." Furthermore, these same sources attest to what the CCC claims: ruining another's reputation (without attempting to change him or prevent danger to others) is a more serious offense than concealing shameful acts.

3. I don't doubt that Clinton feels guilt, wants to be forgiven, is repentant, and hopes for reconciliation, but Catholic tradition does not equate the four. Nor is the relationship between them automatic. Far be it from this sinner to gainsay God's mercy! No, I simply want to say what all of us have learned from our own experience: our sincere sorrow for sin is often not enough for those we have harmed. Human reconciliation is separate from forgiveness and involves considerations of justice and charity, including the need for some kind of restitution.

4. I think discussions of punishment are colossally misplaced. Not because they might exclude charity (this may or may not be true). I

think we need a nuanced understanding of the limits of charity, but more especially the wider exigencies of justice as restitution. What is our appropriate response to the transformative and liberating justice to which God may be calling us? Perhaps Starr (or Clinton) should pay for Clinton's secretary's legal bills. Rather than covering or uncovering infidelities, we need more frank discussions of gender justice, equity, and broken relationships. It is this kind of call for justice that I found lacking in the Declaration. This is why I didn't sign it. But I remain glad that others did.

Accountability
in and for Forgiveness

GLEN HAROLD STASSEN

Many who signed this Declaration are my good friends, and we agree on what matters. I want to agree with them on this matter, too. Yet I cannot sign this statement.

Where Two or Three Are Gathered in My Name

My reaction to the early leaks from the Starr investigation that Bill Clinton had this problem was to believe sadly that it was probably true *and to hope his pastor and his church would help him face the problem, work on repentance, and develop a new life of faithful discipline.* I not only hoped his church would do this for him; I prayed for it. So I am strongly in line with the authors of the Declaration on the theological and ethical understanding of repentance.

When President Clinton first admitted publicly that he had engaged in a sexual relationship, and that he had lied, and had hurt people, I felt relief as well as sadness. It was good that he was finally admitting it. Of course, like others, I wished for a deeper expression of repentance. I prayed that his church was providing him a small group where he could confess and repent more openly, and where he could get help establishing a new, faithful discipline.

Then when I saw a sound byte from the President's deeper confession at the Prayer Breakfast, I hoped that he was getting some help from an accountability group in his church. There was a sentence on the Internet indicating that he was seeking and receiving some pastoral help. But the sentence was understated and unemphasized, and the media failed to pick it up — not until Pastor Gordon MacDonald announced it to his church. I thought that was proper: he should seek pastoral help but not make a big deal of it in the political arena. The Prayer Breakfast is inevitably a mixture of the prayerful and the political, and I thought it would have been appropriate if he had been more explicit ("here is the discipline that I am entering into") and had described an accountability process. It would have been appropriate at the Prayer Breakfast; more appropriate in a church context; exactly appropriate for his pastor to explain to the church. So when Pastor Gordon MacDonald explained it to *his* church, I thought that appropriate. There needs to be some public indication of the repentance and accountability process that Bill Clinton is participating in.

I prayed that, to come through with its responsibility, the church would follow Matthew 18:15-20, would offer a committee for receiving confession and repentance, for discipline in confronting his problem and establishing discipline and faithfulness for the future, and for pronouncing him restored if and when it seemed right.

> "If your brother sins against you, go and show him his fault, just between the two of you. If he listens to you, you have won your brother over. But if he will not listen, take one or two others along, so that every matter may be established by the testimony of two or three witnesses. If he refuses to listen to them, tell it to the church; and if he refuses to listen even to the church, treat him as you would a pagan or a tax collector.
>
> "I tell you the truth, whatever you bind on earth will be bound in heaven, and whatever you loose on earth will be loosed in heaven. Again, I tell you that if two of you on earth agree about anything you ask for, it will be done for you by my Father in heaven. For where two or three come together in my name, there am I with them." (Matt. 18:15-20, NIV).

Notice that Matthew 18:15-20 includes verses 18-20, not usually quoted in individualistic churches: the church has the responsibility to bind and loose, to be prophetic in the sense of speaking on God's behalf. There is a double accountability here: the church must call its members to accountability, and the church is accountable to God for how it does this. I agree wholeheartedly that grace must not be allowed to be cheap grace. Repentance requires a turning and a new way of discipleship. This is not only the responsibility of the individual sinner; it is also the responsibility of the church as *koinonia* (community) to help people repent, turn, and enter into a new way of discipleship. Furthermore, the church is called not only to preach and celebrate the sacraments or ordinances but also to be a community that practices what Jesus commands.

I hope and pray that the three pastors who have agreed to serve in this role will do so in a faithful way. By the very nature of their pastoral work, they are pledged to confidentiality. We cannot know what they are hearing or how they are confronting; we cannot know what disciplines they are imposing; we do not know what leverage they have. I don't believe that we may judgmentally imply that they are failing to confront, failing to impose a discipline, failing to provide the guidance that Bill Clinton needs. If the Declaration is judging that this pastoral process is weak and permissive, or manipulative and insincere, then I urge that we not judge when we do not know.

The Declaration says: "While we affirm that pastoral counseling sessions are an appropriate, confidential arena to address these issues, we fear that the publicity announcing such meetings in order to convince the public of the President's sincerity compromises the integrity of religion." This puzzles me. To my knowledge, the meetings were not announced by the White House, nor has it said anything about them. The nation did not learn about the meetings until Pastor Gordon MacDonald reported his activities to his church. Then the media deluged the three pastors, asking for an explanation. The pastors agreed that Tony Campolo should issue one written statement, and that they would not say more; they have not, as far as I know. Phil Wogaman has remained totally silent. They are in a Catch-22: if they say anything, it will be criticized as publicity; if they say nothing, they will be criticized as they are in the Declaration: "We fear . . ." they are "being called upon to provide authentication for a politically motivated and incomplete repentance that seeks to avert serious consequences for wrongful acts." If they are indeed establishing a discipline that fits repentance, should they announce it or not? I believe they should, and if they do, we should watch respectfully and prayerfully.

We know very little about the structure of the pastoral process.

But inherent in any dealing with a President of the United States is the danger of being co-opted by power and glamor. And there is the danger of the President not staying with the process long enough to confront the underlying demon, receive the needed grace, and establish the necessary new faithfulness. I am not impugning the sincerity of the President's remorse. I mean only that working through the underlying problem will be hard work, and the temptation to drift away will be inevitable when other duties press and the public pressure lessens.

The pastors usually meet with the President individually. I think it wise for them to work as a committee, sharing with one another what they are perceiving and advising. Supporting one another can strengthen their work, their clarity, and their independence from co-optation by the mystique of the presidential office. Surely it would be wise for them to determine that henceforth President Clinton follow the example of the thoroughly and admirably faithful President Harry Truman, and see that his staff always accompanies him and guards him from even the suspicion of scandal. (Truman's biographers have been impressed by his faithfulness and daily thoughtfulness toward Bess, his wife.) How else can the three pastors establish Bill Clinton's accountability to them, and not simply be used politically for the next two years? I suggest that they offer the hope of a declaration of restoration once they observe that Mr. Clinton has worked through the underlying problem and has established a healthy and faithful way of self-discipline — with the ongoing help of others. "Tell it to the church" (Matt. 18:17) can be extended to reporting the good news of restoration to the church.

Mr. Clinton should be asked to commit himself to working toward restoration, and the existence of this discipline process should be made known so that there is a public commitment that supports it, just as a wedding is a public event to show a public commitment supporting the marriage. None of us is perfect; we all need the support and encouragement of others, and we need mutual accountability. The eventual declaration of restoration, if it occurs, should not happen until some time after his presidency is finished, so that it does not become part of presidential politics. The offer of such a future declaration can give Mr. Clinton some hope — and some accountability. If the pastoral process leads to real healing in the life of Mr. and Mrs. Clinton; if it becomes clear over time that the repentance is sincere and the work to follow a new, faithful discipline is real; if a faithful and disciplined life emerges;

if the pastors can sincerely offer a celebration of real forgiveness and restoration four years from now; if the ex-President Bill Clinton can devote himself to do half as much good as Jimmy Carter is doing — would that not be a wonderful testimony to the power of the gospel and the work of the church?

I have a friend who underwent such a church discipline and restoration process. It was hard work, and it was not always happy. He and they were tempted to quit. But it did much good in his life, in his soul, in his inner connectedness, and in his faithfulness. And eventually he was restored. But the key was that it was not only counseling; it was an accountability group whose mission was to bring a report to the church. I am grateful to his church, to the process, and to him for undergoing it, and to God for the redemption that occurred in the process.

The Rule of Civil Decency

In my lifetime, I believe that we have had six or seven Presidents who committed adultery prior to or during their presidencies. I believe that four or five others were sexually faithful. Both political parties are well represented in both groups. It has been the agreed *rule of civil decency that the sex lives of politicians, and certainly of Presidents, was not proper material for politically partisan discussion.* My lifelong, loyal Republican father believes that that civil rule was wise and should be reinstated now. I am grateful that government investigators did not splash the details of the other five or six presidents in the nation's face. Not because it is inconvenient or uncomfortable, but because it becomes a cause for moral cynicism and moral degradation for children, youth, and adults.

The exit polls at the congressional elections indicated that the voters disapproved of Congress's handling of the investigation by a margin of 65 to 31, and of its move to impeachment by 62 to 34. Before these data were in, some pundits interpreted the President's continued — and even increased — high job rating, while his personal rating plummeted, as a popular conviction that the President's sexual actions and cover-up do not matter as long as the economy is doing well. These polling data show that that cynical reading was superficial and wrong. The people are saying that it was inappropriate to metamorphose the investigation of Whitewater into an investigation of sex. They are upholding the traditional rule of civil decency: the sex lives of presidents is not proper material for political discussion. Consider the evidence: 1) The ratings of the President as a person have dropped to half of what they used to be; this means that people do care about his personal misconduct. 2) The ratings of Kenneth Starr are very negative; the people believe that it was wrong to shift the topic of the investigation from Whitewater to Lewinsky. 3) The job rating of the President is about twice his personal rating; the people are saying that the job rating should not be attacked by charges about this sexual matter. 4) The people do have a sense that this investigation and the release of all the voyeuristic material are a departure from the rule of civil decency — and thus wrong, distasteful, and partisan.

Please notice how I am using poll data. I am not saying that polls tell us what is permissible. I am concerned about the morality of the people's interpretation of what has been happening, and I am concerned about the impact on morality of this public dragging through the mud. If we encourage the belief that people do not care about morality as long as the economy is okay, we encourage untruth: it is not what people are saying. And we encourage cynicism about morality, a secular game we should not play.

The reason for the traditional rule of civil decency in public discourse is that doing this in public is a bad example for the morality of everyone — children, youth, and adults. First, the presidency is a bully pulpit; this political use of sex in public transforms the message of his pulpit from overcoming racism, for example, to practicing sexual unfaithfulness. The Declaration is surely right in its concern "about the impact of this crisis on our children and on our students." Second, the political use of public sex inevitably becomes highly partisan. The salacious details are trumpeted for partisan purposes, and truth and wisdom are hard to find in the midst of emotional and manipulative partisan debate. The country and the policy process become highly polarized, and impartial judgment by the prosecutor, the congressional committee, and Congress are almost impossible. Kenneth Starr's support in Committee and Congress comes from the party that opposes the President.

Third, sex scandals dominate the media, the work of Congress, and the work of the President. Citizen groups that work hard to bring other issues of justice before the people cannot get attention in the media because of the attention devoted to salacious issues. The President cannot focus the attention he should on what we should be doing after welfare reform, or to crucial leadership for the economy of struggling nations in Asia, or for world peace. Congress fails to pass campaign spending reform as it crowds the whole budget debate into the final week, with little discussion. The President's intention to make this a year of national dialogue about overcoming racism, which we sorely need, was as overwhelmed by the emotion of this scandal as a Nicaraguan village overwhelmed by a Pacific Ocean tidal wave. Who knows what other important issues got overwhelmed or slighted because the attention of the government, the media, and the people were overcome by this all-dominating sex scandal? Some may say that President Clinton's unfaithfulness is worse than that of the six presidents I have in mind. That does not alter the points I have made. It is still bad for the nation's morality, for nonpartisan cooperation, and for attention to crucial problems that need leadership. It would have been just as tragic for the nation's attention to have been focused on the smaller sexual scandals of those other presidents.

Presidents, like anyone else, should be liable to suit for sexual harassment. But, as with military personnel who are overseas in the armed services during wartime, suits of this nature should be postponed until after their military service is over. Suits disrupt the crucial responsibility of leadership too greatly.

When President Clinton expressed anger that the public investigation was pushing into his private life, and urged us to get on with the work of governing, I agreed. I was raised in a political family. My father had an office in the Eisenhower White House. As part of my training to be a Christian ethicist with a specialty in political ethics, I studied the presidency extensively, and even taught a course on the presidency. I realized that breaking the rule of civil decency would be very destructive for a civil society.

I strongly agree with Gabriel Fackre: "The President's various public professions are an acknowledgment of his accountability to specific standards of fidelity and truth telling, especially the letter he sent to his Southern Baptist congregation, which puts the matter squarely in Christian context. This uniquely *religious* dimension of "repentance" sends us to the New Testament understanding of *metanoia*. It has to do with an "about-face," like that of a prodigal who turns around and makes his way back home with penitent heart and confessional word. Reflecting that reversal of direction, a long tradition in the church con-

153

strues repentance as a threefold movement: contrition of the heart, confession of the mouth, and satisfaction by hands and feet. The last is the visible sign of a turnaround, the intention and effort to make amends for harm done, one that lends credence to the invisibilities of the heart and the audibilities of the mouth."

Fackre affirms that the President has taken the first two steps. The question is whether he is taking the third — making amends and, I would add, entering into a new discipline of faithfulness. We do not yet know the answer to that. We cannot now judge. Probably the heart of the Declaration is its assertion that the President denies his liability for his sin: "When the President continues to deny any liability for the sins he has confessed, this suggests that the public display of repentance was intended to avoid political disfavor." The President has acted, the Declaration says, "with the aim of avoiding responsibility for one's actions." I wonder if this is really accurate. I thought that the President accepted liability and responsibility for his actions, and said he had much work to do with his family to make up for the sin. I took his entering into the pastoral process to be accepting liability, accountability, and, I hope, discipline. He has already paid a high price. His legacy in history has been deeply damaged; his ability to govern has been hurt; his shame has been published and televised for the world to see; his standing as a person has been severely cut down; he has agreed to pay $850,000 in damages to Paula Jones; and he may yet face a court trial beyond whatever Congress does.

But he does believe that Kenneth Starr has sharply partisan and hostile motives, has used his power wrongly for partisan reasons, and has thereby hurt not only Clinton but also the work of the government and the United States. Surely it is appropriate for him to defend himself against this powerful attack. Could it be that his defending himself against the attacks by Kenneth Starr and the Republican Congressional leadership, and his sense that they have crossed the line of civil decency, is what the writers of the Declaration have perceived as denying liability for the sins he has confessed? Could it be that he is not denying liability but defending himself against attack?

I have read of a Korean political leader who expressed remorse for his participation in military violence against demonstrators during the time of authoritarian rule, resigned, and went into seclusion for a year of meditation and atonement — at some financial cost to himself. It was well received. The Declaration is right that repentance requires action to set things right. I hope we will see that Bill Clinton's work with his own family, with the pastors, and with his post-presidency work will show accountability and action to atone for his sin. Only the future will tell. He could yet resign, as the Korean leader did. I have argued privately that he should. A colleague of mine replied that that would be a reward for those who have brought this immorality so salaciously into public and partisan discussion. It would be to encourage similar attacks on leaders in the future. My colleague, too, was sensing the need for defending the rule of civil decency. I think it more likely that the President will stay in his job, and I hope that his actions will show his accountability. Jesus and Paul teach us not to judge, but to take the log out of our own eyes and to welcome one another.

Truth telling, on the other hand, is indeed a proper and crucial question for public discourse. Gabriel Fackre rightly says: "As the Declaration asserts, the functions of government, eminently so its highest office, require trust in professions of truth. Behind legal talk of perjury lies the unspoken — and sometimes spoken — covenant: 'I am telling the truth.' In traditional Christian teaching, the need for the state as an 'order of preservation' against the disorders introduced by human perversity presupposes the responsible ordering of speech. False witness undermines the capacity to govern." We have been in a battle for truth telling by public officials especially since the time of the Vietnam War. It is enormously important for the health of our society and for justice. But here again is the two-sided nature of this sordid affair: Clinton lied when he was asked about his sex life, but he was driven to do that by the collusion of Kenneth Starr's investigators, who gave the line of questioning to the prosecuting lawyers in the Paula Jones case. Neither side should have done what it did. I wish the Declaration would have pointed out the injustices on both sides.

Public and Private under the Lordship of Christ

Many of us have devoted much of our teaching to overcoming the public/private split. We oppose the secularizing split that says the gospel gives no guidance for the public struggle for peacemaking, justice for the poor, the sacredness of human life, and the common good of the beloved community. To say that Christ is Lord over the private life alone and not over all of life, or that the gospel gives no guidance for

155

public life, causes secularism because it teaches us that we should not consult Christ when we shape our work lives, our cultural lives, our educational lives, our civic lives. It teaches that Christ has nothing to say and is not relevant because all that is left is secular authorities. The resulting public secularism also undermines morality.

That secularizing split concentrates Christian ethics on private morality, while ignoring public ethics. When that happens, Christians who should care about justice in all of life ignore it. They vote for candidates who are professed Christians, or are sincere, or good on issues of private morality, while not measuring their *policies* by the Biblical plumbline. Paul Freston, a sociologist in Brazil, has reporting on what has happened when evangelicals came to political power in Latin America and elsewhere. It has been disastrous. Evangelicals have not learned the need for checks and balances against self-righteousness and doctrinaire authoritarianism and thus have produced self-righteous rulers who have been authoritarian, dogmatic, divisive, and insensitive to others' viewpoints. Evangelicals have concentrated on private morality and avoided political and economic ethics.

By contrast with Freston's account is the much more praiseworthy example of Jimmy Carter, whose Christian faithfulness led him to focus world attention on human rights for people being victimized throughout the world. Also praiseworthy was Senator John Sherman Cooper, whose Christian faith and ethics led him to courageous leadership against racism in ways far ahead of his Kentucky constituency then.

The reality of the issue before us is both private and public. Half the issue is President Clinton's sexual unfaithfulness, initial deceitful cover-up, and eventual confession and request for forgiveness. The other half is the public decision by Kenneth Starr to move the investigation from Whitewater to the travel office, to other issues — on all of which he has finally declared he found nothing to prosecute — and then finally to Monica Lewinsky, and to report all the sexual details. And the decision by Linda Tripp to lure Monica Lewinsky into being taped secretly and then to make those private tapes public. And the decisions of leaders from the opposite party to publish it all and move to impeachment. Both halves trouble me deeply. They have troubled the nation greatly.

I am not able to sign the Declaration because it focuses only on the one half. It puts the blame on Clinton, where much blame belongs.

But it puts no blame on the policy decisions of those who nominated and selected Starr, on Starr's policy decisions, and on the policy decision to proceed with the impeachment process. This puts all the emphasis on the private half — sex and cover-up — and ignores the policy half. Are we falling unconsciously into the private/public secularizing split? Are we focusing only on the more private half and ignoring the policy half? Are we thus allowing ourselves, unintentionally, to function as a part of the game defined by the accusers?

This is surely ironic. The Declaration comes from people who share with me the desire to overcome the private/public secularizing split. Yet the Declaration focuses only on sex and cover-up and ignores the policy sins of those who have made this such a salacious public issue. In addition, while we are asking Bill Clinton to repent, it is appropriate for us to repent. In a declaration on repentance and forgiveness, it would be fitting to confess our own sins. I do not see a mention of the log in our own eye in this Declaration

Reinstating the civil decency rule against dragging sex lives into the public arena requires a recognition of different spheres of life — the political and the private — when it comes to partisan public discussion of sex. This is the opposite of the public/private secularizing split that most of us oppose. I want private life and public life to be under God, transformed and guided by faith, responsible for justice and faithfulness in all relations. For the sake of setting a healthy moral example for private life as well as effective leadership in just and ethical policies, I urge us not to drag the sex lives of politicians into partisan politics.

It is like the inappropriateness of dragging the faith of candidates into the public discourse: "Do not vote for Kennedy — he is a Catholic," or "do not vote for Jimmy Carter — he is a born-again Southern Baptist." We want their faith to affect their ethics and their policies, as in Jimmy Carter's leadership for human rights and John Kennedy's peacemaking initiatives. We want it to be expressed on the policy level, and not in attacks on their church membership. In order to overcome the secularizing public/private split, we have to expect faith to be expressed in policy arguments that can appeal to people of different faiths, and not in attacks on people's faith.

Glen Harold Stassen

An Act of Accountability:
Exorcising Racism and Bringing Us Together

Abraham Lincoln was our theologically and ethically most profound President. Like Bill Clinton, Lincoln was raised Baptist and poor in a Southern border state (Kentucky, which resembles Arkansas in many ways). He, too, experienced tragedy in his life. And eventually there was redemption and restoration — in his soul and in his participation in the church. His struggle against the racism of his time lifted us above self-righteousness and into the beginning of the repentance and mutual forgiveness that we so needed, and still need.

Abraham Lincoln took on racism and was assassinated. John Kennedy took on racism and was assassinated. Bobby Kennedy took on racism with more commitment than John Kennedy did, and was almost sure to be elected President before he was assassinated. Martin Luther King took on racism and was assassinated. Bill Clinton has begun to take on racism, and there has been an effort to assassinate him politically. His prosecutor was nominated by the former Dixiecrat segregationist Strom Thurmond; and the Congressional leaders who have backed the prosecution represent that part of the South that did not distinguish itself by taking on racism. Many of them adopted a "Southern strategy," thus using code-word wedge issues to get their party elected. I hate to write these words, but I fear they need saying if we are to deal with our sin.

Any historical outcome has multiple causes. Bill Clinton brought this on himself by his own behavior. That is surely a major cause of this sordid mess. But there are other causes as well. I fear that one factor is a kind of repressed hostility by some against those who take on racism.

Our nation went through deeply emotional divisions during the years of the civil rights struggle and the subsequent years of implementation and nonimplementation, and then retrenchment. We needed to go through that pain. Otherwise we could be now where South Africa was a few years ago. But in the process much polarization occurred. Many have been left with repressed guilt. We have desperately needed a President with the eloquence of a Lincoln, a Kennedy, a King, a Reagan, or a Clinton, who would bring us together, unite us, help us forgive one another and ourselves, help us say: "We have gone through a very painful time, and a very necessary time. We have taken some significant steps in combating racism. Many of us have learned in that process and

158

have repented in our hearts. All of us have more growing and healing to do."

I want to call us to a national celebration, too long delayed, that we did pass the laws that we did, that we did move forward through the valley of segregation and hatred. I want to call us to a national reconciliation with one another, a mutual confession of sin, a mutual forgiveness, and a dedication to walk on the journey to becoming, in fact, one nation, under God, with liberty and justice for all. Presidents who have the eloquence, the feeling, the soul, the heart, and the commitment to lead us in that direction are rare. Those who could have led us there were killed. Therefore, we have never exorcised the repressed guilt and healed our wounds. I wish that President Clinton could use his own now public sin to transform his last two years and our nation into a nation not of self-righteousness and blame but of accountability and forgiveness. We need a new birth of freedom and of community.

Has Faith a Healing Word?

DONALD W. AND PEGGY L. SHRIVER

Was President Clinton's behavior with Monica Lewinsky morally wrong, disappointing and disgraceful, crude and tasteless, rash and stupid? *All of the above!* As two people brought up on and committed to fidelity both before and throughout marriage, we don't take convincing on any of those adjectives. But we detect in ourselves temptations to smugness and self-righteousness that threaten our attempts at Christian humility and a "There but for the grace of God go I" spirit. We know that "all have fallen short of the glory of God"; we are tempted to add, "But at least as concerns the Seventh Commandment we haven't fallen *that* short!" Then we remember . . . there are nine more.

Perhaps the most disappointing quality of this Declaration is its relative scarcity of reference to theology, which is supposed to be the foundation of Christian ethics. The spiritual and political depths of the case of kingly crime, enshrined in Israel's Psalm 51, do not surface in this statement. One would expect more theological profundity from these fellow scholars.

We know, as do the authors of the Declaration, that the Christian response to rightful divine judgment is repentance. Throughout the document there is an assumption that, not only has President Clinton sinned egregiously, but he has not actually repented. He is merely using the religious language of repentance for his own political purposes — a "politically motivated repentance." Perhaps the authors have some unusual access to Clinton's heart and mind that we do not have that assures them that he does not really mean those words. More reliable, we

160

suggest, are the words of Scripture: "Man looks on the outward appearance, but the Lord looks on the heart" (1 Sam. 16:7).

How do we know whether or not Clinton's repentance is real? Possibly his future behavior will be our best clue. But even then *we* can't be quite sure, because like all Christians before God, together we confess that "I do not do the good I want, but the evil I do not want is what I do" (Rom. 7:19).

For the sake of discussion, one might argue whether, sincere or not, public repentance has some value. In the Roman Catholic tradition, the church makes a distinction between "contrition" and "attrition." "Contrition" is from the heart, profoundly acknowledging one's sinful behavior; "attrition" is a pragmatic act that one might call repentance "for political advantage." Traditionally, this lesser repentance is still of some value, is still recognized as better than no repentance at all. Since the authors of the Declaration have already condemned this pragmatic, self-protecting approach as a debasement of religious concepts and have declared that real, heartfelt repentance has not occurred in President Clinton, what ought the President to do? Simply say, "No comment, it's between God and myself"?

From this assumption of false or conniving confession, which arrogates more knowledge to the authors than seems possible, the suspicion grows that religious people who at least allow for the possibility that his repentance is significant and sincere are themselves being manipulated, or "seduced by power." Again, how can we know that those who attended the Religious Leaders' Prayer Breakfast on September 11, 1998, were lured by power and not by compassion? That they were co-opted by presidential power and not by the hope that faith might have a healing word for a leader and nation in serious trouble? (That it became a focus of media hungry for another new angle on a hot story is hardly surprising.)

We thoroughly agree that the offer of forgiveness does not relieve the forgiven person of the consequences of wrongful behavior. Responsibility must be acknowledged and accepted, some acts appropriate to the deed must be undertaken as restitution where possible, and some punishment must be received as recognition of judgment. That President Clinton has denied "any liability for the very sins he has confessed" does not square with reportage of the facts. He has apologized to his family publicly and to his staff privately for having gravely misled and misused their loyalty; and he has signaled a readiness for some official public rebuke. He has already endured *global* scorn and ridicule. He has been subjected to the humiliation of public laughter, voyeurism, and shock at the lurid details exposed in the Kenneth Starr report. Granted that he stupidly allowed his concupiscence to overwhelm decency and moral behavior, he has certainly suffered serious consequences already — and will throughout the rest of his life. As the Declaration suggests, we are likely to have many divergent views concerning what further actions are appropriate.

Like the authors of the Declaration, we are convinced that "politics and morality cannot be separated," but we do believe that they can be distinguished. We live in a society that prides itself on having established a separation between church and state, so that religion cannot easily be made a hostage to whatever politicians may choose to say it is. If religion were as readily threatened by the manipulations of politicians — including the President — as the authors seem to fear, then religion would be dead by now.

Morality in the context of this document seems to stand on two feet: sexual uprightness and truth-telling integrity. Like the authors, we are deeply disturbed by the telling of lies, such as the television appearance by the President when he looked directly at us through the camera and said he had had nothing to do with "that woman." That was a lie, as it turns out, and he hurt his relationship to the public when we learned it was a lie. One danger of lying is that, when one does speak the truth, it may not be believed. If he is truly sorry, many will not believe him. President Clinton may be convinced that his Baptist upbringing allows him to draw that extremely fine line between sexual intercourse and his sexual activities and to claim he did not have "sexual relations." His legal advisers may see that "casuistic twisting of language" as sharp and clever, but most of us see the distortion of truth here. On this moral ground Clinton has a lot of climbing to do to get out of the hole he has dug for himself.

This is indeed a particularly "teachable moment" for the American public to think about the meaning of morality. We have had more public debate on what constitutes sexual moral behavior in the past year than most of us have heard over decades. Indeed, we should be concerned about the impact it has on our children. We were particularly incensed that Kenneth Starr chose to produce an almost pornographically explicit report that undermined the effort of parents to do a careful, age-sensitive interpretation of events. The nearly automatic decision of Congress and the media to publish all of it and to put the Clinton grand jury interrogation video on television was also guided not by wise moral judgment but by "political advantage."

The furor over sexual misconduct and the lie that pleaded innocence has obscured the broader, richer Christian understanding of what constitutes public morality. Our Christian faith is concerned for all our neighbors as well as ourselves, so the "public good" and "public interest" are uppermost concerns of religion toward politics. Defining what is the "public good" — as well as defining the meaning of a "moral society" and "moral leadership — and mediating its varied interests is a major task of religion and of politics.

Children are being educated to an understanding of sexual misbehavior as the chief, if not only, element of morality about which religious people can become exercised. What about Jesus' concern for "the least of these" who are hungry, in prison, cold, and homeless? Huge issues of genocide, warfare and aggression, poverty, environmental decay, racial prejudice, the crisis in public education, global financial turmoil, the critical need for campaign finance reform, the lack of adequate health care for millions, and the precariousness of Social Security — all these have intense moral aspects to them. The word *morality* is itself being debased by the limits this Declaration puts on its meaning. When people say they want to get the Monica Lewinsky affair "behind them," they are saying that it's time to reaffirm the broader meaning of a "moral society." Seldom do we feel so attuned to the general public will as we did in the 1998 fall elections, when the American public said repeatedly, "We are concerned about health care, education, Social Security — not about impeachment." Morality is composed of many values, and these values themselves need to be weighed and balanced at times.

Like those who crafted the Declaration, we share a concern for the abuse of power; but we would again like to expand the discussion beyond what the document selects. Almost in passing, the Declaration comments, "We grant that other parties share guilt," but it offers no specifics. President Clinton, of course, abused his power both in his sexual misconduct and his attempts to block an investigation of it. We would nominate Kenneth Starr as an abuser also, especially if he did in fact allow leaks of information from a supposedly secret grand jury investigation. His report, as already noted, abused its role in vengeful, unnecessary prurience. The "independent counsel" concept has itself become an abusive power, unregulated even in the enormous sums of money spent — partly through Clinton's intransigence and partly through Starr's overreaching. Constitutional limits must be set on this Grand Inquisitor approach in the future. The media have admitted some abuse of power, while continuing to demonstrate it, even as the public screams, "Enough already!"

Another candidate for abuse of power is Monica Lewinsky. Recognizing the sexual Achilles' heel of the President, she connived to employ the powers of youthful feminine sexuality to the service of her own advancement by "aiming at the top." Although the President obviously had greater responsibility for what transpired, she was not merely a pawn. Those who ignore her role as an abuser of power are dismissing women as though they have no capacity to be moral agents. She is in many ways a tragic figure, but one with culpability, too.

Our final observation, like that of the document itself, is to recognize that parts of the public will differ as to the suitable next steps to be taken, because there are many different "public interests." The recent fall elections have been analyzed and will continue to be analyzed in many distinct and even clashing ways. That each segment of the public — the elderly, minorities, the poor, parents and school children, political hopefuls of every stripe — has its own reading of the election returns is understandable, and each segment is likely to read them according to its own interests. Of particular significance is the steadfast loyalty of African-Americans to the President, who has championed that community's concerns more than most other recent leaders. Their search for racial justice is itself a moral issue not to be ignored, and that aspect of President Clinton's moral leadership has reason to be affirmed. So is his continuing effort to improve the health care system in this country, as many of the elderly on Medicare or the poor on Medicaid would affirm. That, too, is moral leadership. Yes, it is a "political agenda," but one with ethical significance.

Christians are called on to seek not only their own self-interest but the good of the nation. Here a serious debate may well be in order. Is a lengthy impeachment proceeding, with the aim of clarifying the moral issues involved and meting out justice, good for the nation? Is a resignation, clean and swift, good for the nation? Is a congressional rebuke and continued work on the tough issues good for the nation?

Back in 1988 our national government faced a Constitutional crisis under the name "Iran Contra." Many citizens and many political scientists considered this violation of constitutional distribution of responsibility for foreign policy a more serious threat to the republic — a higher "crime and misdemeanor" — than was at stake in Watergate. Yet Congress and the public agreed in a broad consensus that the impeachment of another president, fourteen years after Watergate, was not in the national interest. Those who believed the Reagan White House to be innocent in this matter were, in our judgment, politically naive. With Oliver North as scapegoat, the nation passed through this crisis — probably to the larger national good.

It is not clear from the Declaration whether the authors are as disturbed by the charge of perjury against the President as by the charge of sexual misconduct. The latter, for some of us, is the more serious offense for the nation, but legally it is not an impeachable one. Perjury is a serious matter, and Congress is right to focus chiefly on it. But even here, one must ask if every perjury, on any subject, is equally weighty. The President did not with this lie commit treason or bring the republic into imminent danger. It is perhaps on this judgment that we most disagree with authors of the Declaration. All political and moral judgments, of course, are fallible — as are ours.

But, like the authors, we continue to hope that a wise solution will emerge, or will have emerged, by the time this is published. The country at present seems to have concluded that "he has suffered enough," that it is time to forgive and get on with the burdens of governing in challenging times. So far, we tend to agree.

PART III

National Columnists Speak Out

A Chance to Reset Our Moral Course

STEPHEN L. CARTER

So what should Bill Clinton do? Everyone now knows that he had an intimate relationship with a 21-year-old White House intern and spent seven months lying about it — to the public, to his family, and to investigators. His presidency is so hobbled that when United States armed forces attacked terrorist targets in Afghanistan and the Sudan on Thursday, many Americans wondered whether the President just wanted to distract the public from the scandal. Commentators, not all of them on the right, are talking of impeachment or resignation.

Yet throwing in the towel or toughing it out are not the President's only choices. It may be that the Monica Lewinsky scandal presents Mr. Clinton with two much-needed opportunities: the opportunity to finally change his own life and the opportunity to help the nation regain its moral bearings.

In the current uneasy moment there is a chance for genuine moral rejuvenation, which the nation desperately needs. And President Clinton can help lead that process, although he will first have to convince the public of his determination to turn over a new leaf. True repentance begins with a forthright and nonaccusatory admission of wrongdoing.

The President and his defenders continue to argue that his relationship with Ms. Lewinsky is a private matter. But this notion is morally sloppy.

Although the people most harmed by President Clinton's conduct are surely his wife, his daughter, and (lest we forget) Ms. Lewinsky herself, adultery is private only in the limited sense that it should not be against the law. It is wrong for prosecutors, even special prosecutors, to spend public resources trying to ferret it out.

But once adultery becomes publicly known — by whatever means, fair or foul — it is too late to raise the privacy argument. Adultery rips at the fundamental fabric of marriage itself and thus is ultimately a public wrong.

This does not mean that adultery is unforgivable — any more than lying itself is unforgivable. But when the President's defenders announce that the American people are prepared to forgive him, they are stating only a possible truth, not a settled fact.

The question is whether President Clinton is prepared in his heart to be forgiven. The President, as an evangelical Christian, surely understands that the premise of forgiveness is true repentance.

Apology and acceptance of responsibility (the two matters that have obsessed the news media in recent days) are only a part of what is required. True repentance is not a public relations strategy. True repentance requires a determination to turn and walk the path of good.

What would count as evidence of true repentance? For one thing, Mr. Clinton must abandon his habit of resorting to legalism and obfuscation. Far better, if Mr. Clinton wishes to set a moral example, would be a magnanimous confession of this weakness and an explicit promise to do right. Second, the President owes concrete apologies, not only to his family, but to the many surrogates he sent forth to defend him, to Ms. Lewinsky and to the American people as well. Third, Mr. Clinton and his supporters must put an end to the lashing out, as though others are to blame for this humiliation.

This may seem a hard standard, especially when so many other characters in this drama have also behaved in ways that are immoral. Linda Tripp, for example, pretended to be a friend who would keep Ms. Lewinsky's confidences, but she was not. In short, she lied.

And Kenneth Starr himself might have behaved in a more honorable fashion had he not let his zealous pursuit of President Clinton outstrip his sense of decency. I suspect that most prosecutors, faced with evidence that a married man lied under oath to cover up an affair, would respond: "Call the National Enquirer. This is not the kind of work I do."

Indeed we, the people of the United States, have not acquitted ourselves admirably in the contretemps. If the polls are correct, we do not really care very much whether the President lies to us as long as we are otherwise happy with his performance. This alarming display of cynicism teaches our children that what matters most is not right or wrong but simply getting what we want.

President Clinton, in his handling of the current scandal, has tended to reinforce rather than challenge this dangerous cultural trend.

This does not mean that Mr. Clinton should resign, despite the steady drumbeat to that effect by many politicians and editorial writers. Unless Mr. Starr's report contains convincing evidence of other serious misconduct, Mr. Clinton may be able to serve out his term with dignity. But he must exercise genuine moral leadership. His address to the nation on Monday night, conveying only the merest hint of contrition, did not come close.

True, most of our Presidents have been morally tarnished in one way or another, and many have committed adultery or lied to the nation or both. But Bill Clinton is the President under today's rules, when what was once left unreported is now fair game. And it is his own recklessness, not an unfair standard, that has produced the current crisis.

It may be, as many pundits have complained, that we have lost our national capacity for moral outrage — at least as long as the economy is humming along. Even if the current scandal had never arisen, our moral sense has been corroded by the steady drip-drip-drip of everyday lying and cheating.

Still, the President's predicament might be a godsend. It may be heaven-sent for Mr. Clinton himself because sometimes getting caught is the only way to learn the lesson. He will never have a better opportunity to seek the spiritual solace of true repentance. It may also be heaven-sent for the rest of us because sometimes it takes a rude shock to wake the national conscience, which is, in our post-modern era, not defeated but exhausted.

That conscience needs awakening because our sense of right and wrong is ultimately what makes America a special place. This depressing scandal might represent our best chance at reinvigorating our shared belief in an American moral code — the clear understanding of right and wrong that sparked the civil rights movement and won the cold war. A moral code for which we are prepared to sacrifice our own short-term interests, in exchange for the nation's long-term good. A moral code, in short, that matters.

In its place we have set an ethic of selfishness, in which sacrifice is a dirty word, in which successful leadership is measured only by the rise of the S. & P. 500 and in which the only use of words like right and wrong is for political gain.

We have the chance, finally, to turn our national misfortune to national advantage, to restore the proper balance to our politics — so that the quest for electoral advantage or for a place in history is guided by our moral sense, and not the other way around. The challenge for President Clinton is whether he possesses the moral courage to lead us there.

Lies That Matter

ANDREW SULLIVAN

When a country strikes against terrorists, there should be no doubt as
to the motives for its actions. When the President of the United States
addresses the nation to explain a military campaign in retaliation for the
murder of American civilians, there should be no smidgen of a doubt as
to the integrity of his words or the authenticity of his actions.

Commentators last week spoke about America's actions in Sudan
and Afghanistan with a wry smile on their faces. They drew parallels
with Wag the Dog, the film in which a war is invented by spinmeisters
to counter a presidential sex scandal. That any such parallel could cred-
ibly be made shows how far America has sunk in the leadership of the
free world, and how vulnerable Bill Clinton has rendered his country
and its citizens. The threat of terrorism shows, perhaps more palpably
than anything else in a dangerous world, why the President of the
United States needs to be able to be believed, trusted, and feared.

Bill Clinton, after his pathetic, humiliating, and duplicitous address last Monday, showed for the last and most definitive time that he
is none of these things. Which is why he should do the honourable thing
and go now, before the Congress, if justice has any chance, forces him.

Whatever grudging admiration one has for an administration that
has, in fact, conducted America's domestic affairs with a surpassing com-

This essay first appeared in *The New Republic*, September 14 and 21, 1998. It is
reprinted by permission of THE NEW REPUBLIC, © 1998, The New Republic, Inc.

petence, there comes a point in any politician's relationship with his peers and his countrymen when something fundamental has broken down. If the most accomplished British prime minister in history were shown to have lied directly and knowingly to the House of Commons, he would still have no choice but to resign. But in many respects Clinton has done far worse than this. He has lied baldly to his own party, to his own staff, to members of Congress, to the representatives of the legal system, and, in the most direct and unmistakable terms, to the American people. He has lied under oath, and he has lied when he has had no need to whatsoever. He even lied when he semi-apologized last Monday, in saying his testimony in the Jones suit was legally accurate.

Doesn't every politician lie? To an extent, of course. But this man has taken the principle of cynical duplicity to a new and chilling level. I saw it upfront when I heard him describe the events in Bosnia as another Holocaust and then take a poll to decide whether to stop it. I saw it when he said he would do anything to end the scourge of AIDS and then signed a bill that would have thrown every HIV-positive soldier out of the military.

Then there were the meta-scams: the welfare reformer who was eventually forced into it by a Republican Congress and then claimed credit himself (of course); the budget-balancer who was forced into fiscal neutrality by the polls and then claimed it was his proudest legacy; the feminist who routinely treats women as if they are fools, tokens, or sexual objects.

Is it any excuse to say that the final lie that undid him was about something as trivial as consensual extramarital sex? Surely not. To begin with, it is not a trivial act to take regular sexual advantage of a young employee in the workplace. It is an act of almost pathological recklessness. And if the man cannot confess to such a stupid, sordid dalliance, what hope is there that he'll tell the truth about campaign finance? Or his motives for bombing Afghanistan? If he cannot bring himself to apologize fully, even when he has dragged the entire country and dozens of innocent people into a legal and political morass for seven months, and even when the entire political class is virtually begging to let him off the hook in return for unmitigated contrition, then the truth is he has lost all contact with the meaning of moral responsibility, if not reality itself. And then he had the gall to plead for a new zone of privacy for himself and his family and to enjoin us to repair the fabric of the nation. The narcissism of the man beggars belief.

But perhaps the deepest level of cynicism came in what the administration leaked about Hillary Clinton, who, we were told, had found out about the affair just three days before. The only conceivable response to this was to laugh until you burst a blood vessel. This was the woman who knowingly sat by her husband while he lied about Gennifer Flowers in the 1992 campaign. This was the woman who took the lead in attacking Kenneth Starr days after the Lewinsky scandal broke in January, describing him as part of a vast right-wing conspiracy. And this was the woman who spent most of last weekend prepping her husband for what might well be perjurious testimony and then co-wrote the defiant speech he delivered on Monday night. At what point does one begin to balk at this kind of cynicism and to regard it not simply as contemptible in itself but as a corrosive force in the culture as a whole?

Yes, we knew much of this before. We knew he could hardly tell the truth about his golf scores when we re-elected him. But that re-election was based on a spurious gamble: that economic results matter more than political character. What Americans did not count on in 1996 was what making such a moral compromise would do to the character of the man in question.

America's moral insouciance allowed Clinton to believe he could get away with almost anything. Which is why he shamelessly corralled shifty businessmen through the White House in return for illegal campaign dollars, chatted on the phone with Dick Morris while Morris played footsie with a prostitute, and cavalierly carried on an affair in his very office with an employee half his age. These are the actions of a man who has come to believe he is beyond the moral measure of anyone else and that nobody has the capacity to catch him.

So now that he is caught, it is little surprise that his response is not contrition but outrage. How dare we hold him accountable now, when we have let him off so many times before?

My own bet is that we still don't know the half of it. If Clinton's past is any guide, what the Starr report contains about intimidation of witnesses and encouragement of deceit might make our hair stand on end. Yes, it's petty business. Sex is often a petty business. But honesty in a President is not a petty principle. Without it no system of democratic government can withstand the cynicism and disengagement that will overwhelm it.

Clinton has already done a fathomless amount to define down

America's collective notions of candour, decency, and accountability. If he is shown beyond a doubt to have lied and then is allowed to get away with it, Americans will have gained two years of phoney stability but have lost their constitutional and cultural soul. They will have allowed the chief enforcer of the laws to treat those laws with contempt. They will have tolerated a role model for their children whose definition of morality is whatever he can get away with.

Clinton is a cancer on the culture, a cancer of cynicism, narcissism, and deceit. At some point, not even the most stellar of economic records, not even the most prosperous of decades, is worth the price of such a cancer metastasizing even further. It is time to be rid of it. For good and all. Sooner rather than later.

Baby-Boom Virtue

SHELBY STEELE

Sen. Tom Harkin of Iowa said recently that President Clinton was a "failed human being but a good President." This struck me as a near-perfect formulation of a moral idea that blossomed rather notoriously in my baby-boom generation: that political and social virtue is more important than private morality in defining a person's character. In this ethic, public virtue is in fact a substitute for individual responsibility, so much so that personal irresponsibility may not threaten the essential "goodness" of a person whose politics are "progressive" and "compassionate." It is a baby-boomer sophistication that the politically virtuous person is virtuous.

When Sen. Harkin made his remark, he was inviting us into this sophistication as a way of defending the President. Failure as a human being was no more than an interesting irony because Mr. Clinton was a "good President." If the polls are right — high job approval despite a low view of the President's moral character — my generation's sophistication is now the nation's. How did we get here, and what kind of political culture has it left us with?

To begin with, we baby boomers may be the only generation in American history to have actually won its adolescent rebellion against its parents — to have our case against them prevail. Our parents' generation believed in private morality and had a great, self-sacrificing sense of personal responsibility, but their idea of the "social good" allowed for racial segregation and a constricted role for women in society. If a depression and a world war led them to embrace conformity as a form of stability, it is also true that this conformity led them to tolerate social unfairness and, in the 1960s, to support a questionable war more by reflex than by reflection. By the '60s this self-sacrificing and honor-bound generation found itself identified with America's deepest national shames — racism, sexism, militarism, and an acquiescent conformity that facilitated all of the above.

A New Idea of the Good

So it was the peculiar fate of us baby boomers to come of age at the moment when our parents' generation was losing much of its moral authority. Without a credible authority to tamp down our adolescent grandiosity, we could assume that we represented a new truth. And we could easily see our parents' faith in private morality and responsibility as the source of their hypocrisy and shame.

For us, true virtuousness redeemed society of its shames. Possessing a public morality that stood against all of America's terrible "isms" was the real test of a person's character — not his private morality. In the private realm we made fulfillment the goal and recast personal responsibility as an ordinariness that met only the low standard of a discredited generation.

Thus, in the name of virtuousness that could redeem society and allow for our fulfillment, we created a new "good" in which private moral responsibility was secondary, if not passé. This was a profound mistake that brought a storm of disorder and pain into our personal lives. It is also the mistake that has now come back to ruin our generation's first presidency.

The problem was that we created a virtuousness that could be achieved through mere identification. When personal responsibility is separated from virtue itself, then it is possible to have a much celebrated male feminist who also gropes and harasses women. His feminist credentials are not earned through personal responsibility; they are established by his open support of feminist policies, by his mere willingness to identify himself with the feminist agenda.

178

This virtue-by-identification formula produces ideas that function more as icons of virtuousness than as sound policies. When President Clinton calls for a reading program that will involve a million college-student tutors, I don't think he really means his "solution" to work; I think he means it to show his concern for America's educational crisis. The grandiosity of the program represents the magnitude of virtue that is available to the Americans who will identify with it. His style is to evoke the adolescent energy, idealism, and faith of the '60s as a kind of promise of what identification will bring. In iconographic policies the promises are what count; they open the icon for identification.

It has been the dark genius of Bill Clinton to transform much of our public policy into iconography. If his poll-inspired education policies sound like bumper stickers — "lower class size," "no social promotion," etc. — and do nothing to breach the frozen bureaucracies that stifle education, they do offer the opportunity to feel engaged with the problems. If his "mend-it-don't-end-it" affirmative-action policy is unfair, largely ineffective, and riddled with terrible unintended consequences, it functions well as an iconographic policy that gives the President and Americans generally a chance to identify with racial goodwill.

But iconography of this sort is even more effective in its negative mode. Because it represents virtue, it also licenses demonization. Those who do not identify are not simply wrong; they are against virtue and therefore evil. Any politics of virtue is also a politics of demonization, and this has been a boomer specialty since the 1960s. Only today it is not the over-30s who are mean and extreme; it is the conservatives who tend to believe that true virtuousness — social or personal — is grounded in responsibility and sacrifice.

We could not have had a Bill Clinton without the generational corruption that allowed virtue to be achieved through mere identification. When this is possible, people can — with little more than the embrace of an icon — become the good so that their virtuousness precedes all that they do. Even affairs with interns. When we consider ourselves innocent, Albert Camus says, we "give birth to evil."

Toxic Statecraft

And this is where our boomer ethic begins to spill a certain toxicity into the culture. When you are already good, it is easy to feel that responsibility is redundant and that irresponsibility (bending principles, spinning facts) may actually facilitate virtuousness. With this license you can reshuffle the campaign spending laws or invent a new virtue like "diversity" that lets you assault old principles like excellence and merit. The toxicity in all this reinvention is the destructiveness that accompanies it.

It was Mr. Clinton's ingenuity to elaborate his generation's corruption into a charismatic politics of identification and reflection, of virtuousness and demonology, in which he could be seen as a good and competent President despite the absence of a coherent foreign policy and no domestic achievements beyond those forced on him by the opposition party. But what makes him especially dangerous for the country is all the artful statecraft he brings to the betrayal of responsibility.

PART IV

President Clinton
on the Record

President Clinton's Televised Statement of August 17, 1998, regarding His Grand Jury Testimony of the Same Day

Good evening.

This afternoon in this room, from this chair, I testified before the Office of Independent Counsel and the grand jury.

I answered their questions truthfully, including questions about my private life, questions no American citizen would ever want to answer.

Still, I must take complete responsibility for all my actions, both public and private. And that is why I am speaking to you tonight.

As you know, in a deposition in January, I was asked questions about my relationship with Monica Lewinsky. While my answers were legally accurate, I did not volunteer information.

Indeed, I did have a relationship with Miss Lewinsky that was not appropriate. In fact, it was wrong. It constituted a critical lapse in judgment and a personal failure on my part for which I am solely and completely responsible.

But I told the grand jury today, and I say to you now, that at no time did I ask anyone to lie, to hide or destroy evidence, or to take any other unlawful action.

I know that my public comments and my silence about this matter gave a false impression. I misled people, including even my wife. I deeply regret that.

I can only tell you I was motivated by many factors. First, by a desire to protect myself from the embarrassment of my own conduct.

I was also very concerned about protecting my family. The fact that these questions were being asked in a politically inspired lawsuit, which has since been dismissed, was a consideration, too.

In addition, I had real and serious concerns about an independent counsel investigation that began with private business dealings twenty years ago, dealings, I might add, about which an independent federal agency found no evidence of any wrongdoing by me or my wife over two years ago.

The independent counsel investigation moved on to my staff and friends, then into my private life. And now the investigation itself is under investigation.

This has gone on too long, cost too much, and hurt too many innocent people.

Now, this matter is between me, the two people I love most — my wife and our daughter — and our God. I must put it right, and I am prepared to do whatever it takes to do so.

Nothing is more important to me personally. But it is private, and I intend to reclaim my family life for my family. It's nobody's business but ours.

Even presidents have private lives. It is time to stop the pursuit of personal destruction and the prying into private lives and get on with our national life.

Our country has been distracted by this matter for too long, and I take my responsibility for my part in all of this. That is all I can do.

Now it is time — in fact, it is past time to move on.

We have important work to do — real opportunities to seize, real problems to solve, real security matters to face.

And so tonight, I ask you to turn away from the spectacle of the past seven months, to repair the fabric of our national discourse, and to return our attention to all the challenges and all the promise of the next American century.

Thank you for watching. And good night.

Transcript of President Clinton's Speech at the Religious Leaders' Prayer Breakfast, September 11, 1998

Thank you very much, ladies and gentlemen. Welcome to the White House and to this day to which Hillary and the Vice President and I look forward so much every year.

This is always an important day for our country for the reasons that the Vice President said. It is an unusual — and I think unusually important — day today.

I may not be quite as easy with my words today as I have been in years past, and I was up rather late last night thinking about and praying about what I ought to say today.

And rather unusually for me, I actually tried to write it down. So if you will forgive me, I will do my best to say what it is I want to say to you. And I may have to take my glasses out to read my own writing.

First, I want to say to all of you that, as you might imagine, I have been on quite a journey these last few weeks to get to the end of this, to the rock bottom truth of where I am and where we all are. I agree with those who have said that, in my first statement after I testified, I was not contrite enough.

I don't think there is a fancy way to say that I have sinned. It is important to me that everybody who has been hurt know that the sorrow I

185

feel is genuine — first and most important, my family, also my friends, my staff, my Cabinet, Monica Lewinsky and her family, and the American people. I have asked all for their forgiveness. But I believe that to be forgiven, more than sorrow is required. At least two more things: First, genuine repentance, a determination to change and to repair breaches of my own making. I have repented.

Second, what my Bible calls a broken spirit. An understanding that I must have God's help to be the person that I want to be. A willingness to give the very forgiveness I seek.

A renunciation of the pride and the anger, which cloud judgment, lead people to excuse and compare and to blame and complain. Now, what does all this mean for me and for us?

First, I will instruct my lawyers to mount a vigorous defense using all available, appropriate arguments. But legal language must not obscure the fact that I have done wrong.

Second, I will continue on the path of repentance seeking pastoral support and that of other caring people so that they can hold me accountable for my own commitment.

Third, I will intensify my efforts to lead our country and the world toward peace and freedom, prosperity and harmony. And in the hope that with a broken spirit and a still strong heart, I can be used for greater good, for we have many blessings and many challenges and so much work to do.

In this, I ask for your prayers and for your help in healing our nation. And though I cannot move beyond or forget this, indeed I must always keep it as a caution light in my life. It is very important that our nation move forward.

I am very grateful for the many, many people — clergy and ordinary citizens alike — who have written me with wise counsel. I am profoundly grateful for the support of so many Americans who somehow, through it all, seem to still know that I care about them a great deal, that I care about their problems and their dreams.

I am grateful for those who have stood by me and who say that, in this case and many others, the bounds of privacy have been excessively and unwisely invaded. That may be. Nevertheless, in this case, it may be a blessing because I still sinned. And if my repentance is genuine and sustained, and if I can then maintain both a broken spirit and a strong heart, then good can come of this for our country, as well as for me and my family. (APPLAUSE)

The children of this country can learn in a profound way that integrity is important and selfishness is wrong. But God can change us and make us strong at the broken places.

I want to embody those lessons for the children of this country; for that little boy in Florida who came up to me and said that he wanted to grow up and be President and to be just like me. I want the parents of all the children in America to be able to say that to their children.

A couple of days ago when I was in Florida, a Jewish friend of mine gave me this liturgy book called "Gates of Repentance." And there was this incredible passage from a Yom Kippur liturgy, and I would like to read it to you.

"Now is the time for turning. The leaves are beginning to turn from green to red to orange. The birds are beginning to turn and are heading once more toward the south. The animals are beginning to turn to storing their food for the winter.

"For leaves, birds and animals, turning comes instinctively. But for us, turning does not come so easily.

"It takes an act of will for us to make a turn. It means breaking old habits. It means admitting that we have been wrong, and this is never easy. It means losing face. It means starting all over again. And this is always painful. It means saying I am sorry. It means recognizing that we have the ability to change. These things are terribly hard to do.

"But unless we turn, we will be trapped forever in yesterday's ways. Lord help us to turn from callousness to sensitivity, from hostility to love, from pettiness to purpose, from envy to contentment, from carelessness to discipline, from fear to faith.

"Turn us around, oh, Lord, and bring us back toward you. Revive our lives as at the beginning. And turn us toward each other, Lord, for in isolation, there is no life."

I thank my friend for that, and I thank you for being here. I ask you to share my prayer that God will search me and know my heart, try me and know my anxious thoughts, see if there is any hurtfulness in me and lead me toward a life everlasting. I ask that God give me a clean heart, let me walk by faith and not sight.

I ask once again to be able to love my neighbor — all my neighbors — as myself, to be an instrument of God's peace, to let the words of my mouth and the meditations of my heart, and in the end, the work of my hands, be pleasing. This is what I wanted to say to you today. Thank you, God bless you. (APPLAUSE)

Contributors

Don S. Browning, Alexander Campbell Professor of Religious Ethics and the Social Sciences at the University of Chicago, is the author of.*From Culture Wars to Common Ground: Religion and the American Family Debate* (Westminster John Knox, 1997).

William J. Buckley, Visiting Scholar at the Center for Clinical Bioethics, Georgetown University Medical Center, is the author of "Public Theologies in an Age of Ethnic Rivalries," *Catholic World* 237 (Nov.-Dec. 1994).

John P. Burgess, Associate Professor of Systematic Theology at Pittsburgh Theological Seminary, is the author of *In Whose Image: Faith, Science and the New Genetics* (Geneva Press, 1998).

Stephen L. Carter, Professor of Law at Yale University, is the author of *Civility: Manners, Morals, and the Etiquette of Democracy* (Basic Books, 1998).

Jean Bethke Elshtain, Laura Spelman Rockefeller Professor of Social and Political Ethics at the University of Chicago, is the author of *Augustine and the Limits of Politics* (Notre Dame University Press, 1998).

Gabriel Fackre, Samuel Abbot Professor of Christian Theology Emeritus at Andover Newton Theological School, is the author of *The Doctrine of Revelation: A Narrative Interpretation* (Eerdmans, 1997).

Contributors

Stanley Hauerwas, Gilbert T. Rowe Professor of Theological Ethics at the Divinity School of Duke University, is the author of *Sanctify Them in the Truth: Holiness Exemplified* (Abingdon, 1998).

Robert Jewett, Harry R. Kendall Senior Professor of New Testament Interpretation at Garrett-Evangelical Theological Seminary, is the author of *Saint Paul Returns to the Movies: Triumph over Shame* (Eerdmans, 1998).

Fr. Matthew L. Lamb, Professor of Theology at Boston College, is the author of *Toward a Theology of Transformation: Solidarity with Victims* (Crossroad, 1982).

John Lawrence, Professor of Philosophy Emeritus at Morningside College, Sioux City, Iowa, is the author of *Fair Use and Free Inquiry: Copyright Laws and the New Media* (Ablex, 1989).

Troy W. Martin, Associate Professor of Religious Studies at St. Xavier University, Chicago, is the author of *By Philosophy and Empty Deceit: Colossians as a Response to a Cynic Critique* (Sheffield Academic Press, 1996).

Donald W. Shriver, Jr., William E. Dodge Professor of Applied Christianity Emeritus and former President of Union Theological Seminary, New York, is the author of *An Ethic for Enemies: Forgiveness in Politics* (Oxford University Press, 1995).

Peggy L. Shriver, former Assistant General Secretary for Research of the National Council of Churches, is the author of *Having Gifts That Differ: Profiles of Ecumenical Churches* (Friendship Press, 1989).

Lewis Smedes, Emeritus Professor of Christian Ethics at Fuller Theological Seminary, is the author of *Standing on the Promises* (Nelson, 1998).

Klyne Snodgrass, Paul W. Brandel Professor of New Testament Studies at North Park Theological Seminary, is the author of *Ephesians* (Zondervan, 1996).

Max L. Stackhouse, Stephen Colwell Professor of Christian Ethics at Princeton Theological Seminary, is the author of *Covenant and Commitments: Faith, Family and Economic Life* (Westminster John Knox, 1997).

Glen Harold Stassen, Lewis B. Smedes Professor of Christian Ethics at Fuller Theological Seminary, is the author of *Just Peacemaking: Ten Practices for Abolishing War* (Pilgrim, 1998).

Shelby Steele, of the Hoover Institution, Stanford University, is the author of *A Dream Deferred: The Second Betrayal of Black Freedom in America* (HarperCollins, 1998).

Andrew Sullivan, a senior editor at *The New Republic*, is the author of *Love Undetectable: Notes on Friendship, Sex and Survival* (Knopf, 1998).

Edward P. Wimberly, Jarema Lee Professor of Pastoral Care and Counseling at the Interdenominational Theological Center, Atlanta, is the author of *Moving from Shame to Self-Worth: Preaching and Pastoral Care* (Abingdon, 1999).

Nicholas P. Wolterstorff, Noah Porter Professor of Philosophical Theology at Yale University, is the author of *Art in Action: Toward a Christian Perspective* (Solway, 1997).